NEXT ACT, GIVE BACK

DISCOVER YOUR PERSONAL PATH TO GO FROM BEING CHARITABLE TO BEING A CHANGEMAKER

By Kirsten Bunch

Kirsten Bunch Initiatives, LLC
P.O. Box 692
Ringwood, NJ 07456

Ordering Information:
Special discounts are available on quantity purchases by corporations, associations and others. For details, contact the publisher at the address above or email info@kirstenbunch.com.
Events:
The author is available for keynotes, workshops and coaching sessions. For more information or to book an event, contact info@kirstenbunch.com.

Efforts have been made to verify information contained in this publication. The author nor the publisher assumes any responsibility for errors, inaccuracies or omissions.
This publication is not intended to be legal or accounting advice. All readers are advised to seek competent lawyers and accountants to follow laws and regulations.
The reader of this publication assumes responsibility for the use of the information. The author and publisher assume no responsibility or liability whatsoever on the behalf of the reader of this publication.

ISBN-13: 978-0-692-19868-1
ISBN-13 Ebook: 978-0-692-17083-0

Cover by Monira Mussabal
Interior images by Piere d'Arterie
Images of Author by Nina Pomeroy Photography
Printed in the United States of America
Library of Congress Control Number: 2018911847

I never set out to do peace work. My passion has always been racial justice. But, one of my most formative life experiences was that my college boyfriend shot and killed his best friend on our campus. So, I lost a friend who died and I lost my boyfriend to the prison system.

I was pastoring a very small congregation that owned 40,000 square feet of space in one of the most expensive places in the country to live. They had named their dream for their contribution to their neighborhood as being creating peace in the midst of violence.

So, we got together a bunch of nonprofits that are on the frontlines. We said, "would there be value to you in having a shared space and greater opportunities to collaborate?"

There was a resounding yes.

When we started talking in 2009, the problem was violence in the streets and the lack of opportunity that led to that violence. Now it's just a flat-out gentrification and displacement crisis.

We've lost 25 percent of the African-American population in what was historically a predominantly African-American community.

What happens if the immigrant justice folks, the Black Lives Matter folks, the folks who are working to increase minimum wage so that people in the most expensive rental place in the country can afford to stay where they have grown up, begin to collaborate?

That's kind of the dream.

It's clear that my own story led to this moment in some ways that I didn't realize as it was unfolding.

I couldn't have done it by myself, or I would never have tried to do it by myself.

-Sandhya Jha, Oakland Peace Center

Oakland, California

Dedication

This book is dedicated to all the women, girls, boys, men and genderqueer people who have seen problems in their communities and acted to make change. It's for the activists, journalists, artists, writers, politicians, scientists, academics, celebrities, techies, stay at home parents and students who believe in healthy, safer and equitable communities, and work to make change happen.

This book is dedicated to the people of all races, religions (or no religion), ages, professions, those in every social-economic status and abilities who embrace love over hate and have ideas to create a better world.

This book is dedicated to my friends and colleagues from all over the world who work tirelessly and often at great sacrifice to themselves so that people can live with dignity, fresh air, full bellies and nourished minds.

This book is dedicated to my mom who showed me what it means to push boundaries and to move past fear. And to my dad who encouraged me to always reach for my next act and to never be ordinary.

This book is dedicated to my wife who has stuck with me and always supported me through month-long work trips away from home and my own personal reinvention. You show me how to show up in this world with tenacity, love and adventure.

Finally, this book is dedicated to the woman and her child that I met that day on Chicken Street in Afghanistan and all women like her. It wasn't your job to teach me a life lesson, but you did, and I am grateful.

Author's Note

I typically work with people who self-identify as women. However, some of my clients self-identify as men. I celebrate that my clients have their unique gender identifications. My use of the terms "woman" and "women," as well as the corresponding gender pronouns, are not meant to exclude but to reflect where I am on my journey to understand better how to incorporate more inclusive language in my work.

CONTENTS

Introduction:
Someday is Now

"Power: the capacity or ability to direct or influence the behavior of others or the course of events."
- Oxford Dictionary

I understand what it's like to see a human being suffering and to do nothing. Not because I didn't care. Because I didn't know what to do and I didn't believe that I had the power to do anything.

In 2006, I was walking down Chicken Street in Kabul, Afghanistan. I was exploring the small, family-owned shops that line the street and sell local handcrafts, jewelry and carpets. My colleague and I were trying to get a feel for the craft traditions of the country.

We were in Afghanistan doing some legwork for a women's economic development project. The goal of the project was to help women in Afghanistan build businesses, so they could have an income, feed their families, send their kids to school and in general, have more control over their lives.

After spending an hour or so going in and out of the stores on Chicken Street, I came out of one and a woman wearing a blue burka approached me. I hadn't interacted much with a lot of women during the short time I had been in Afghanistan, and it felt pretty foreign to me to have this woman who was completely covered from head to ankle, with a mesh square surrounding her eyes, edge nearer to me. She stood not directly in front of me but off to the side a bit, careful not to block my path. She put out her hand to ask for money.

A baby, probably six or seven months old, lay in her arms. The baby was nothing but a skull. His cheeks were sunken, and his eyes appeared too big for his face. Her child was starving to death. She was probably starving to death, too.

I looked at the woman and then at her baby, and I kept walking. I didn't do anything. I didn't give her anything. I didn't help her.

I was afraid of her. I was afraid of the baby. I was afraid of what the woman and her baby told me about myself…that I was powerless to help her.

I thought she was asking me for what I couldn't give. I could have given her money. I could have bought her food. What I couldn't give her was the life that she deserved. The life where her baby was healthy and strong. The life where she spent her mornings at home laughing as her baby played in the morning sun that filtered through her kitchen window.

> *Who was I to help this woman? What did I know about her situation? What did I know about what she needed? What right did I have to think I could do anything to help her?*

I felt powerless to help her because I didn't know how to help. I heard the words in my head: "Poverty and suffering are inevitable." I knew it didn't accomplish anything to just give money. She probably would have to hand it over to her husband, brother or someone else who controlled her life. These were stupid words based in fear and powerlessness. I didn't know how to change her life, so I did nothing. Worse, I didn't believe that I *could* do anything. Who was I to help this woman? What did I know about her situation? What did I know about what she needed? What right did I have to think I could do anything to help her?

I'll never forget that woman and her child. I can still see them. I can still see her hand stretched out to me. I think about what my inaction says about me and wonder why, after so many years, do I still think about them? It can't be as simple as that I am a terrible person or have no compassion. The actions I have taken throughout my life tell me that's not true. I keep returning to the lack of awareness I had of my own power. I thought anything I did to help would not have helped them. That's the only reason I've come up with after all these years.

I'm writing this book because I believe if someone had said to me in 2006 when I met that woman and her baby, "Kirsten, you don't have to keep walking. You don't have to be ashamed or afraid that you don't know what to do. It's normal to wonder if you have any power to change that woman's life. I assure you, you do. Let me show you how," I would have done something to change her and her baby's life and I would have changed my life in the process.

This book is for you if you think you can do more than give a little money to charity and volunteer a few hours of your time, even if you have no idea what that might look like. I know you have ideas to transform lives in your community. You just don't believe (yet) that you have the power to do so.

I'm writing this book because you come to me at cocktail parties, at the gym, in the grocery store, at roller derby practice, at charity events and you tell me, "*Someday,* I'm going to 'give back.' I have this idea for a nonprofit, a business, a community art project that can change lives, and when I quit my job/retire/save enough money/win the lottery/clone myself, I'm going to make it happen." You have told me your ideas for how you will, someday, stop dogs and cats from languishing in shelters, use your money to invest in world-changing ideas, protect your community from the effects of a changing climate, create a public art program to revitalize your city, or support new minority teachers to adjust, adapt and confront a lack of diversity in their schools.

While you wait for someday, our kids are being gunned down in their schools. Women's reproductive rights are at serious risk of being controlled by men in power. Your transgender colleague is being fired because he finally decided to show his true self. Communities are on the verge of collapse because of rising sea levels. And you are missing out on the opportunity to walk a path in life that has deep personal meaning, and that will transform how you show up—in your life, at your job, in your family and in your community.

I know this, not because I'm trying to be an alarmist or to make you feel badly, but because I have lived it and continue to find my own path of deep personal meaning and transformation. I can see the *power* you have to change your community and to change lives, including your own. Someday is now. Because if it's not now, someday will never come.

You have ideas. Now you need to take action. Let's get started.

How This Book Will Help You

This book isn't about establishing a nonprofit, business or foundation, or establishing anything at all. The specifics of your idea are not the point. You can use this book to solve a family problem if that is the change you want to make in the world.

> *Giving back doesn't have to mean returning a gift to others. It can mean giving back to yourself. It can mean giving back to the dreams of how you were going to make a change in the world as a young college graduate.*

Giving back doesn't have to mean returning a gift to others. It can mean giving back to yourself. It can mean giving back to the dreams of how you were going to make a change in the world as a young college graduate. Or, giving back to yourself the permission to be a little selfish to go after what you really want—be it a more soul-feeding career, relationships that make you joyful instead of drained or using your voice to tell your story. When people say they want to give back, I find that what they mean is they want to help others. What I *feel* when they say that, is they want to heal themselves by taking on a loving role in their community. There is no more powerful motivation than that.

I hope you will use this book as a starting point, not as a to-do manual. It's not meant to be a prescription for how you help people. As my good friend told me when she was reading a draft of my manuscript, before I had completed the book, "I don't know if I want to start a project in my community, but I've found clarity in how I can find my path forward in my life where I can feel powerful and whole." Finding your inner superhero, your shadow, isn't about rescuing someone else; it's about becoming aligned with who you are so that you find your place among your community, from a place of reciprocity, not heroism. This book is about living a life that aligns with who you want to be. It's about using your *story, dreams and ideas* to write your legacy. It's about healing yourself by creating things in the world (a career, a passion project, a song, a way of being) that you are proud of and that feeds your spirit. It's about looking at how you interact with your community and your world, not through the lens of guilt, denial or heroism, but through a lens of pride, awareness and mutuality.

What is Next for You?

Perhaps you have come to a reflection point in your career and life. You've moved mountains and built empires. You've run marathons and companies. You've put hundreds of stamps in your passport or thousands of miles on your minivan, or both.

Your kids are grown and going off to college or to travel the world, and you've come to the painful realization that they aren't coming back. Your identity as "Mom" has shifted beneath your feet. You feel conflicted between the joy caused by your kids flying into adulthood and the grief you feel at the loss of the role you held in their lives for so long.

Maybe retirement has come into view, or the writing is on the wall that you have given all you can to your current business or career. Maybe you are only 10 years into your career, and you know the path you are on is not right for you. Maybe you are happy where you are in your life and career and want to go even deeper to create even more meaning and personal fulfillment.

Whatever stage you find yourself in at this moment, you are asking yourself, "What's next for me?"

You feel that your life's work is not done. Even after all your accomplishments and successes, you have more to do. Or you feel incomplete. My clients tell me all the time that they feel like something is missing. Hopefully, through these pages, you will see what the future can be if you step up and in because history tells you that you have what it takes to change lives. You want to play a part in building a better world.

Now, it's a matter of focusing. Clearing space for your next act, perhaps the most crucial act. The one where all the skills, networks and wisdom you've battled to learn and build over the years combine to form your superpower. Your superpower that will first change the direction of a young person in trouble, or a community that's gone off the rails, and then will strengthen to change the lives of thousands of young people or light the way for hundreds of communities to find peace and justice.

Those lives you touch might never know all your great life accomplishments. They might not see that you earned a graduate degree or sat in the corner office. They and those who come after will only see that crucial chapter, the most important one. The one where you believed that you had the power to create change in your community and took action.

And the world needs you to make a change. Look around you. Shit's going down. You notice it. You feel it, like a punch in the gut when you drive by those boarded-up buildings and know that your idea for a healthy, affordable community grocery store would help revitalize that neighborhood. You feel an electric spark when you stare out the window with your cup of coffee in hand and dream of young women going off to college pursuing studies in technology. Your program was what first got them interested in technology and told them that their interests would be encouraged and supported for the rest of their lives when they were only in the sixth grade.

"But, wait!" you say. "I mean it when I say as soon as I have enough money in my 401(k), I'm going to do it. Someday will come!"

Here's how I know that if someday is not now, it will never come.

Because you don't need to have money in your 401(k) to put action behind your idea. Research doesn't cost a thing. Talking to people impacted by the problem you want to address doesn't come out of your 401(k). It's free to tell people in your network about your idea— even if it's half-baked. Especially if it's half-baked because then they get a chance to be a part of your creative process. They get to contribute, and that makes them vested. That makes them more likely to support you and your idea, with money, introductions, information and time.

I am so energized by the women who book free discovery calls with me who are ready to take action on their desire to create change in their lives and their communities. I can usually tell 15 minutes into the conversation if I am speaking to a Changemaker. How? Because Changemakers don't talk about reasons why they *can't* do something. They may talk about the obstacles that are in their way, but they also ask me to help them overcome those obstacles. I think of a

Changemaker as somebody who *acts* to make change in their community. For them, *someday* has arrived and they are ready for it!

"Someday" comes for the people who put small, micro-actions behind their idea today, because otherwise, *something* will always get in the way. There will always be an excuse for why "someday" isn't here yet. As my business coach and friend, Robyn, says, "Procrastination is the enemy of change."

More people than ever are stepping up to create grassroots initiatives to take action to fix problems in their communities, countries and the world. Friends, neighbors and colleagues are organizing protests and movements to stand up against violence, hate and inequality.

Traditional nonprofits are adapting and morphing into nimbler models able to embrace opportunities and create services and programs focused more on constructing sustainable and resilient communities instead of providing Band-Aid™ solutions.

The opportunities and methods for creating social and environmental change have exploded over the past decade.

Social enterprises, B Corporations, impact investing, and social venture capitalism are embracing innovation and technology to create a new landscape for doing good in this world.

- Social enterprises use business principles to bring about financial, social and environmental impact in markets and communities where traditional markets and government are not meeting the needs of all people. Social enterprises can be for-profit, non-profit or a hybrid. VisionSpring, an organization that brings affordable eyeglasses to millions of people, is an example of a social enterprise.

- B Corporations (Benefit Corporations or B Corps) are certified businesses that balance profit and purpose; they measure their performance by social and environmental indicators that are as important as financial indicators.[1] Twenty-nine U.S. States recognize B Corporations as a legal form of a corporation, and there are 2,000 B Corps in 140 industries in 50 countries.[2] Patagonia and Warby Parker are certified B Corps.

- Impact investing is an investment strategy used to generate social and environmental returns in addition to financial returns. It's a rapidly growing industry that allows you to invest your money in alignment with your values. For example, Ellevest, founded in 2016 by social change maven, Sallie Krawcheck, helps "you reach your goals by investing up to half of your portfolio in companies that power positive social change by advancing women."[3]

- Venture Philanthropists are nonprofit investors who raise philanthropy to back companies whose products and services are changing lives in underserved communities. Acumen, founded in 2001 by former "Wall Streeter," Jacqueline Novogratz, invests in early-stage companies whose products and services enable the poor to transform their lives.

Could You Change One Life?

You are asking the question, "What can I do?"

Here's my answer.

Anything you want.

You've got power to make real change in the world.

How do I know? Because ideas are powerful, and I know you've got ideas. So, I know you've got power.

You don't have ideas? I beg to differ.

Let me ask you this. Have you ever looked outside your door, or your car window, seen a problem and thought *someone ought to do something about that?*

Only to have a few ideas and questions run through your mind… "What if?" "I wonder how that would work?" "How about if we?" "Why don't they?"

> **What if your idea is the one that changes everything ?**

But then that little voice in your head starts talking (the voice inside you that tells you your ideas are stupid, that no one will listen to you, that you don't know what you are talking about).

Girl, you don't know how to fix that problem! No one wants to hear your idea. Just give some money to that charity, and you're good as gold. They'll fix that problem.

But what if your idea is the one that changes everything?

What if your idea is the one that keeps that kid from hating her body so much that she can't think about anything else? That stops dangerous chemicals from seeping into your town's water supply? That changes the way your neighbors feel about welcoming refugees into your community?

What if?

That big, world-changing idea of yours is not going to change anything if it stays tucked away in your notebook or on your computer. That's a fact.

But where do you start? I'm going to show you. In the following pages, I am going to walk with you and help you see your power. I'll give you questions at the end of each chapter to help you think more deeply and start your journey of becoming a Changemaker in your community.

I have spent 25 years working to make a difference. My work has taken me to 30 countries on five continents.

> *Everyone has the power to live a life full of meaning and personal fulfillment and to create a better world.*

I've designed and managed social impact projects in 10 countries that helped change the lives of millions of people. I have helped raise more than $20 million for non-profits and social enterprises that are disrupting markets and changing how we look at charity.

As I worked alongside some of this century's leaders in creating environmental and social change, I have learned one very important lesson:

Everyone has the power to live a life full of meaning and personal fulfillment *and* to create a better world.

I know this because I've seen people like you—corporate executives, business owners, entrepreneurs, stay-at-home moms, artists and academics—change their lives while helping create safer, healthier and more loving communities.

I've seen a CEO of a mid-sized company step forward to say, "enough!" to poisonous farming practices. I've worked with an engineer turned soccer mom who established an organization to help girls grow up to become scientists. I've watched a small business owner mobilize her community to end bullying after her daughter committed suicide at the age of twelve.

None of these people are celebrities or politicians. They are ordinary people making extraordinary change in their communities.

> *But, when you live your legacy, when you dig deep into a problem now and play your part in finding a solution to create a better world, when you contribute in a way that will have a ripple effect in your community, you won't just feel good; you won't just help people: You will be transformed.*

I am surrounded by people who have changed their lives and are working to change their communities. I have seen the metamorphosis that my clients go through when they step into their role as Changemaker.

Don't you want to **live** your legacy, instead of simply *leaving* a legacy? The difference is light years apart. When you leave a legacy, by bequeathing money to an organization or cause in your will, you'll feel good. You'll feel like you've done something to help people in your community. You'll imagine that your gift will be put to work to help people and hopefully you'll be remembered, at least for a little while. That feels good.

But, when you *live* your legacy, when you dig deep into a problem now and play your part in finding a solution to create a better world, when you contribute in a way that will have a ripple effect in your community, you won't just feel good; you won't just help people: You will be transformed.

You will find new purpose and passion in your life. You will no longer wonder what mark you have left on the world. You won't have to ask the question, "What have I done to make a difference?" You will feel it every single day. And it won't just feel good; it will be life-affirming.

My Story

My story isn't a big one. I haven't found a cure for cancer. I haven't ended the war in Syria. I haven't won a Nobel Prize, an Oscar or any award for that matter. I didn't graduate from Harvard or Stanford with all the networks and privileges that come with those degrees. I'm pretty ordinary. But I have always had the dream to improve my world, to be part of a community of people who see that with empathy and compassion, we make the world a place where all people want to live.

For most of the past 25 years, I have worked for international non-profit organizations. My career has spanned many different roles and geographic locations. I managed programs for exchange students in New York City. I organized activities for grassroots volunteers in Costa Rica. I managed events for foreign dignitaries in places like Istanbul and New York. I ran a summer program for underserved kids in a mountain-top village in Mexico. I started a design center for women entrepreneurs in Kabul, Afghanistan. I worked with a team in Michoacán, Mexico on a movement to remove the use of dangerous lead in pottery production.

I also helped raise money for programs that allowed women in poverty to start businesses so they could feed and clothe their children. I have designed and have written grant proposals that helped bring eyeglasses to millions of people in communities in Bangladesh so losing their near-vision in their 40s didn't mean an end to their ability to earn a living. I have brought teams of environmental experts together to design conservation programs in places like Ecuador, Peru, Nicaragua and Costa Rica.

I've traveled to 50 countries and have met thousands of people of all different races, religions, cultures and income levels. I've had experiences that a naive girl raised in upstate New York could never have imagined.

My life and work have been full of contrast that has left me, at times, speechless with tears of pain or joy (sometimes both) running down my face.

I walked through a village in Burkina Faso (a country in West Africa) and held the hands of small children with the swollen bellies of malnutrition while showing them a video I had just shot on my fancy new tablet of their mothers enthusiastically whirling around in a welcome dance.

I dined on rich food and wine on the balcony of the home of the director of a powerful, global foundation in Cairo, Egypt while looking over the city where more than 30% of the people live in poverty.

I saw the elegant beauty of Bangladeshi women in vibrant, colorful saris sitting on the dirt floor, threading raw silk onto a spinning wheel in a dark, dusty weaving factory. Their male colleagues smoking cigarettes in the next room, filling the factory with toxic smoke and creating the chance for a loose ash to ignite one of the fabric scrap piles and start a potentially life-ending fire.

I accepted stew from a mother living in a dirt-floor shack in Guatemala, knowing that she saw it as a point of pride that she could feed her guests, and also knowing that her children would probably have to go without meat that day or maybe even that week. The choice of choosing the mother's dignity over her children's full bellies was not lost on me. (It was a choice I struggled with every time I was invited into a family's home where food and clean water were a daily struggle. But, I couldn't say no. I would often take a few bites and pass my bowl to a child to share, trying to be mindful of the mother's pride and the kids' bellies.)

I have witnessed the pain and suffering caused by poverty, violence, greed and inequality, poisoning humans, animals and the natural world. I have experienced the hopelessness of antiquated cultural and religious rules that keep girls and women locked behind doors, both literally and figuratively, destroying any chance of them contributing their full potential to the intelligence, creativity and beauty of the world.

I have been places where there was no electricity, or running water, where women cooked over open-fire stoves inside small rooms that filled with toxic smoke. I have been in homes where children lived with ailments that could easily be cured by a trained doctor. And I have slept in a dingy hotel where I could hear the young woman in the next room beg her "John" not to force her to have anal sex.

As a queer woman, I've personally experienced hatred and violence directed at me by other people. As a survivor of sexual abuse, I've directed hatred and violence toward myself. I've personally caused great pain in my own life and the lives of others.

But I've also witnessed and experienced pure joy, love and innovation.

In Mexico, I watched as a grandmother taught her young granddaughter how to craft a clay pot the way her grandmother had taught her, knowing that her granddaughter wouldn't face the same health problems that she had. Her family, with the help of the organization I worked with, *Barro Sin Plomo*, had removed lead from their pottery making process.

As an outsider looking in, I saw a truer sense of community than I had ever seen before. Women, who were so poor that no bank would let them in the front door, came together to form savings groups through their own banking system. They encouraged each other to create a financial safety net for their families and loaned each other money to start new businesses.

One of my favorite memories is visiting a community in Burkina Faso where the women had collectively saved enough money to buy a corn grinder for the village, so they could spend less time manually grinding corn and more time tending to their small businesses and children. They were so proud to show us what they had been able to do. We joined all the people in the village for the walk from the center of the village to where the new machine was housed, dancing and singing all the way. The kids peered in through the barred window as the head of the savings group demonstrated for us how the machine worked.

These experiences, and so many more like them, were what made me feel alive. I don't mean alive as might be depicted in a Hollywood movie scene, the one where a happy couple is riding down a sunny country road in a fancy convertible, holding hands with the wind blowing in their hair, relishing in the amazement of life. *"Feeling alive!"*

I mean alive like, "I see you, world. I see how ugly you are. I see all your problems. The cruelty. The hate. But I still love you because I also see the good." I see the old man who cooks food every morning for the street dogs in Bangkok. I see my friend, Awa, who, after her brother was killed in an automobile accident in Senegal, started an international movement for road safety.

———————

My experiences through my work made me feel alive because they took me out of my safe, sterile life in the United States and allowed me to witness the jumbled world that stretched beyond my own community. I learned by taking risks and putting myself in situations that pushed me way beyond what was comfortable and familiar.

I loved it all…building programs and finding money for them. I loved traveling the world and meeting people I would probably never have met if it weren't for my position. I was proud of my work. I had fun. And I couldn't have imagined a better job.

Until I started to hate it. Until I found fault in every job. Then I jumped from one role to the next, always thinking the new job would be better.

But after a "honeymoon" period, I would find fault, and would quickly become unhappy. Normal work problems would feel insurmountable.

I began to question my relevance to the mission of the organizations with which I worked. I deeply questioned whether I had anything to contribute to the problems that I desperately wanted to play a part in solving. I felt disconnected to the mission, the donors and my coworkers. Worse, I found myself not caring anymore.

For a person who has always cared immensely about people and animals and who worries a lot about the problems facing our world, not caring anymore hurt and it was incredibly confusing. It sent me into a tailspin. At the age of 42, I hit an identity crisis head-on.

My identity was wound tightly into my work. But it wasn't my career that I identified with so strongly, it was the experiences I'd had because of my work. It was the wonderful fact that I was privileged to meet so many different types of people, to taste so many different types of food and experience the ways in which people interact with each other and their environment.

So, when I started to dread my work, that was a HUGE wake-up call.

When I was away on a work trip, I couldn't wait to go back home. I lost interest in the places I visited. I realized I was becoming immune to poverty. I suppose in some ways I was experiencing this because I felt completely ineffective like my work didn't have the impact I wanted it to have. I couldn't see that I was making a difference anymore.

But I also felt a deep absence of community in my life. I had been working in others' communities for years, while I barely knew my neighbors. My friends were so spread out across the world that I was quite lonely when I was home.

I remember sitting in a particularly difficult staff meeting. People were angry at each other. Sides had been taken. It was a tough time. The organization had "gained a few pounds" and needed to trim down. We had to make significant cuts to the budget and had laid off a group of people. We had been in turmoil for months.

But we were finding our way through the difficulty. My colleagues on the senior leadership team and I had come up with a solution to restructure the organization, with the goal of making it more efficient and effective. We still had some challenging times ahead, but we were ready to move forward.

I wanted nothing to do with it, and I didn't know why.

Sure, there was a lot of tension, and going to work every day was hard. But there were some really rewarding pieces of the job. However, I was still miserable. This was a deep misery bordering on depression, the kind of misery you feel when something is so off in your life that you can't see clearly.

A couple of years later I realized what was so off. Some might call it a midlife crisis. I call it a crisis of legacy.

I didn't feel like the vision I had for my life was the life that I was living. I was living too safe. In my mid-40s, I was unable to deny the pressure of time. I knew on a very guttural level that I wanted to create something I could point to and say, "I did that. I created that."

To live big. To not play it safe. To try. To take a risk and create *something*. *That* is my legacy.

Of course, I didn't know what that "something" was at the time. That clarity came later, with the help of a couple of great mentors, a loving, supportive, wise group of women and a lot of work.

So, I finally quit my job. I decided that I needed to build something of my own, or at least try. If I didn't try, I would resent it for the rest of my life. I would feel like I was not living my legacy.

I had an idea to start a program where people could grow their community-changing ideas in a creative, supportive environment. But I sat on my idea because I was afraid to start. I didn't know what to do first. I didn't know what it was supposed to look like. This made me restless and frustrated.

Then, the morning of November 9, 2016, the day after the U.S. presidential elections. I turned to Facebook and saw everyone's posts. They said:

"What can I do? I want to do something, but I don't know how to begin."

"I don't want to see my trans friends, my immigrant neighbors, the women in my life disregarded and disrespected. I want to do something. But what? How do I begin?"

In that moment I knew how to help *you* begin. I had been starting social and environmental change programs for 20 years! I knew that if you were serious. IF you were ready to step up and make CHANGE in your community and FIGHT for whatever it is that you believe in, then I could help you figure out how to turn your idea, (or maybe even just your desire to do *something)*, into real change.

So, I started. I sat down and mapped out my idea. And it has been really hard. I was filled with self-doubt and to be honest, I still feel like that sometimes. But then I focus on the people I can help to create change. The kids who need help, the communities who need healing and protection. I focus on the women I meet when I speak at meetings and conferences who tell me how desperately they want to find deeper meaning in their lives. Who tell me they are frustrated because they are not living a life that makes them shine. I have a mission and a purpose, and I don't want anything to stop me. I'm not going to miss out on my chance to help you transform people's lives, including your own.

With that in mind, I kept building. And I got help. I hired a mentor. I found a community to assist me in pushing my idea kicking and screaming into the light.

Two years later, I'm helping my clients turn their world-changing ideas into action and impact; I'm helping them change their lives and their communities. I am launching a group program where women come together to build a powerful, unstoppable community of Changemakers.

How My Goal Will Help You

My goal in my work and in this book is to help women step into the role of Changemaker. I'm thrilled to give you the tools, inspiration and support you need to stop wasting your talents and time on jobs and activities that don't light you up. To help you see how you can use the power you have to instigate positive change.

In this book, you will read inspiring stories of women who are finding deep personal fulfillment in creating heart-centered businesses, organizations and creative projects that are not only changing their communities but are also changing their own lives.

We'll talk about the art of reinvention and the art of changemaking. I'll introduce you to methods and structures to house your world-changing ideas. We'll dig deep into how you show up as a woman who steps fully into her life and legacy instead of waiting for someday.

As I write this, I reflect on all the women and men who see a more powerful version of themselves and who have taken the first step to explore how they can become that person by accepting my offer to have a conversation. It's difficult to express the excitement I felt when a woman by the name of Chana told me how she knows she's meant to follow a career path of creating good in the world, but she wasn't sure what steps to take. Or Larna, who wants to create an educational fund for kids in her community and isn't satisfied with just writing a check to a university but who doesn't know how to make her idea happen. And then there was Monique who told me how she wants to help her 12-year old daughter write a series of books to help black kids with disabilities, like her, realize they aren't alone. I get so excited about these conversations because, regardless of the idea or the situation affecting the person telling me their idea, I believe in them. They've taken the first step to put action behind their idea by booking a call with me. I offer this opportunity to you, too. And I believe in <u>you</u>. If, after reading this book, you are curious about how you can live a life more in alignment with the life you dream for yourself, let's talk. I know it can be scary to schedule a call with someone you don't know. I've been there. I took a leap of faith to book a call with my mentor when I was first starting out. I've never regretted it. With her help and the help and support of the women in her program, I changed the direction of my life. Now, I am doing what I love to do: helping women live lives that light them up and create healthier, safer, more beautiful and more just communities. That's my vision. That's my way of giving back. That's how I have become a Changemaker.

I know I am on the right path when my client Susanne, who is working with high school girls in the Bronx to help them pursue college programs in science and technology, says, "Before I started working with Kirsten, I felt like I was swimming in an ocean with no land in sight. As a result of my work with Kirsten, I feel even more empowered, energized and totally out of the weeds."

Finally, there is Dianne and Tami, founders of Kinona Sport: "Moving the give back part of our business forward has been very frustrating and left us feeling like we are not doing an important piece of our company. After working with Kirsten, we felt more focused and purposeful. We know that we will be able to easily determine which charitable organization best fits with Kinona as a brand, as a personal extension of ourselves, and as something we can embed in our company culture."

These testimonials are social proof that my vision is now a reality.

A few months ago, I started putting a sticky note on the wall in my office with the name of every person I'd talked to who was curious about how they could become a Changemaker. I want to make it easy for you to join my wall because I know as the number of stickies grow, the number of people living fulfilling lives and creating better communities grows.

I've made it easy for you to join the wall. I don't charge money for discovery calls, even though they are valued at $500. All you must invest is 15 minutes of your time. To set up a time to talk with me, simply go to www.kirstenbunch.com/call and find a time that works for you. That's it. I can't wait to help you get started.

How to Use This Book

The Next Act, Give Back Workbook provides you with the space, structure and encouragement to design your next act. I have also included bonus exercises in the workbook that you won't find in the book. You can get your free workbook at kirstenbunch.com/workbook.

I wrote this book to be both motivational and practical. My vision is that people of all ages and abilities will be able to use it to change lives, starting with their own. In it you will find:

- **Inspiring stories** of women and men who, despite their fear and often not knowing exactly what to do, have put action behind their better-world ideas and created powerful change in their communities.

- **My proprietary method** that I designed to help my clients (and now YOU!), create a changemaking life that fits into the reality of your life.

- **A set of thought- and action-provoking questions** at the end of each chapter. These *Go Deeper* questions will help you in your personal exploration of creating your next act as a Changemaker.

To assist you in outlining your vision further, I want to give you a **special bonus**. The **Next Act, Give Back Workbook** provides you with the space, structure and encouragement to design your next act. I have also included bonus exercises in the workbook that you won't find in the book. **You can get your free workbook at kirstenbunch.com/workbook.**

If you are **reading** this book as a member of a book club, community foundation, faith community or school, the book and *Go Deeper* questions translate into powerful group discussions. Please reach out to info@kirstenbunch.com for information on the group curriculum I designed to be used with this book.

Finally, if you have questions or are simply curious about how you can become a Changemaker, book a free discovery call with me. I open up a few free discovery calls every month, and they fill up quickly. You can grab your spot at kirstenbunch.com/call.

Part 1:

Your Next
(and Greatest) Act

CHAPTER 1:

Reinvent (Yourself), Repurpose (Your Skills), Renew (Your Soul)

"Reinvent: To bring back; revive."
- Dictonary.com

While in her 50s, Ruth Sutcliffe was laid off from her job in a fragrance company. From one day to the next, she went from making six figures and having a career that was her identity to having virtually no income and no business card.

Ruth had worked hard all her career. She was a "career woman," a label that these days feels superfluous but was an important marker for women starting their careers in the 1970s and 1980s. One of Ruth's claims to fame was inventing the scent for blue Windex.

Ruth had spent her career putting her ideas, time, energy and passion into her job and she was suddenly, in Ruth's words, "Reduced to no-one." She felt she was "Not worth anything anymore." All the time, passion and hard work that she had put into building her career were gone. Business colleagues she had thought were her friends were gone as well.

Suddenly, Ruth was on her own, without the system, and all its advantages, that she had worked within for over 30 years. Ruth felt like she was dying. She was looking for an opportunity to be alive again, to be relevant and productive but she couldn't clear her mind to realize the first steps that would make her whole again.

Then her mother's health declined rapidly, and she passed away in 2015. Before her death, Ruth devotedly visited her mother in the assisted living facility. During that time, she saw her mother, the nurturer of the family, shoved to the side, her life and her story irrelevant to her caretakers. It frustrated Ruth and broke her heart.

Ruth recognized there was little stimulation for the residents in the assisted living facility, many of whom suffered from illnesses like dementia and Alzheimer's disease. These people had also been pushed aside, just like her mother.

She thought, *if I can do something to help these seniors, I'm going to do it.*

Ruth began to awaken, and a light bulb came on. She asked herself, *how do I use my talents to make life better for people without coming out with another perfume? How do I twist the formula? How do I make my work more important?*

She adopted a new motto *"Humanity versus Vanity."* It represented that she wanted to do something for humankind in a different way. She wondered how she could engage seniors through their sense of smell.

Pulling from her 30 years of working with scents, Ruth began to develop scents that would stir memories in seniors. She was very mindful to develop scents that would resonate with people over 70 years of age and especially focused on creating smells like popcorn and fresh-baked apple pie to remind them of their childhoods.

She began to study how the loss of smell can be a symptom of Alzheimer's and how loss of smell impacts people's appetites. She thought, *wouldn't it be great if we could stimulate these seniors' sense of smell and help them eat better?*

Ruth began to further develop her idea by going to assisted living facilities and hosting "smelling sessions." She developed clue cards to go along with the scents. To date, Ruth has carried out smelling sessions with more than 500 people.

Today, Ruth's *Essential Awakenings™ Smell and Memory Tool Kits* "…elicit conversation and engage in memory recall through the sense of smell." Although designed for people suffering from Alzheimer's and dementia, the "essential smells" have also been an aid in helping one aneurysm survivor regain her sense of smell."

Ruth's dream for her business is to have every assisted living and caregiving agency buy and use a kit. She wants to start a movement to incorporate smell therapy in patients with dementia.

"I know I bring a lot of joy to the seniors. There is nothing more enjoyable and gratifying [than] to see elderly people so happy."

I love that Ruth reinvented herself into a Changemaker, finding deep personal relevance, using what was familiar to create a product that is new and powerful.

Reinvent Yourself

What if, like Ruth, your next act could be something that changes people's lives and gives you deep personal satisfaction, pride and fulfillment? Whether your goal is to leave your current career to focus full-time on changemaking, to create a part-time passion project or to incorporate changemaking into your present business or job, chances are you'll have to do some reinventing of yourself.

> *Reinventing yourself into a Changemaker isn't about starting over. It's about building on what you've already accomplished. It's about stretching yourself to create a career and life that you are excited about and that fits you.*

In this chapter, I am going to ask you to think about what reinvention will look like for you. Specifically, you will want to identify the reasons behind wanting to connect more deeply with your community and your desire to make a difference. You can use the life you have lived so far as a jumping off point of your reinvention. And as you do, you can also explore why you are answering that little voice in your head telling you that something in your life needs to shift.

Reinventing yourself into a Changemaker isn't about starting over. It's about building on what you've already accomplished. It's about stretching yourself to create a career and life that you are excited about and that fits you. Reinvention is also about looking around the world and deciding where your values intersect with where you want to fit in.

There are no rules about what your reinvention must look like. I tell my clients all the time, "If you are going to go through the trouble and the struggle to reinvent yourself, why wouldn't you go bold and create the life you want?"

When I first started working with my client Louise, who had recently left her job at a big corporation, she would tell me she should start a consulting practice to advise corporations on corporate social responsibility because it is what she knew. But I could tell that this didn't really light her up. It was very practical but why leave the security of a well-paying job to do the same thing you were doing, especially if you aren't excited about it? I asked Louise, "If you could impact any issue on the planet, what would you do?" Her answer was, "Protect wildlife." That's what I call finding your North Star. Knowing this, Louise started to build out her changemaking idea that excited her. I'll share more of Louise's journey later.

People reinvent themselves into Changemakers for a lot of reasons. Sometimes it's out of curiosity or a desire to renew their lives or careers. Others are looking for their next challenge to conquer, after building a successful business or raising a family. Some are forced into changemaking because a problem touches their lives so deeply they are compelled to get involved.

In my work with women who want to build their legacy and create transformative change in their lives and communities, I've found five common reasons why they launch into this life-altering journey. Often, my clients cite more than one reason for wanting to become Changemakers. These are the ones I see most often and the titles that apply to the reasons.

1. Their current life doesn't feel like it fits them anymore. (Too Tight Lifers)

2. Their life has been shaken up by a life event. (Shake Ups)

3. They want to up their game beyond donating money and volunteering. (Game Uppers)

4. They want to create a legacy. (Legacy Creators)

5. They are responding to a crisis in their community or family. (Critical Responders)

TOO TIGHT LIFE

When my clients tell me they are being called to reinvent themselves because they feel like their current (or former) career or way of life feels like it no longer fits, I can relate deeply. My motivation for my reinvention was that my old career and life didn't fit me anymore. It was physically uncomfortable for me to spend my time, energy and ideas in a job that didn't fulfill me. I didn't feel like I mattered. That was really painful, and that pain transformed me into someone I didn't recognize and someone I didn't want to be.

Several months ago, I had a discovery call with a woman who had listened in to one of my free webinars. She told me that she lies in bed every night, unable to sleep, thinking about the idea she has to create real change in the world. She hates her job in finance. She feels like her life is ticking away and she's not doing what she is meant to be doing. But, she's afraid. In her 30s, with two young children and an expensive life in New York City, she is afraid to pursue her dream of becoming a social entrepreneur. So, instead of taking even small steps to move her idea forward, she is consumed with "what ifs" and "somedays."

This sounds like a mild form of mental and emotional torture. I know from experience that it is. Like this young woman, I spent many sleepless nights obsessing over one problem or another at work. Worrying about what someone had said or the opportunity that had passed me by, blaming the organization or my colleagues for my unhappiness. But what was really going on was that I was trying to stay and succeed on a path that wasn't right for me anymore.

It may not be that dramatic for you. You may like your job but wonder what else is out there. Or, maybe you love the business you've created and want to make it even better by sharing your success with others. You might see giving back as a logical next step after having built successful businesses or careers.

Many of my clients describe this feeling that something is pulling them toward a different decision as coming from deep in their belly. It might start out as an idea that takes root in your brain at a charity auction when you see someone else transforming lives. That idea grows in your brain and gut until it consumes you and you start to dream of a different future.

Whatever the feeling is for you, I want you to keep this in mind:

You'll never have more time than you do today.

None of us know what will happen tomorrow. Life can change in an instant. If your life is working for you, but you dream of having a deeper purpose, keep reading because I'm going to help you make that happen.

SHAKE UPS

I call people, like Ruth from Essential Awakenings, whose curiosity about becoming a Changemaker was spurred by a major career or personal life event, "Shake Ups."

Shake Ups can be inspired by events like:

- A loss of a job

- A personal illness or death of a loved one

- An empty nest

Being laid off (or fired), especially in your late 40s and 50s, when the idea of finding a new boss is unappealing, is a perfect example. When you have put so much of yourself into a job or company only to find yourself included in the latest layoff, it makes you rethink jumping back into the same pond. Especially if you have some financial flexibility, either through a good severance package or planning.

The death of a friend, colleague or family member, especially someone close to your age, can force you to take a look at your own life and what you are going to do with the time you have left. Your own illness or an accident can cause you to rethink what imprint you are leaving on the world, and whether you are living the life you really want for yourself.

The empty nest is also a catalyst. For years, your time and energy were absorbed by your children. Now they are growing up, busy with high school activities or have already gone off to college. They still need you, of course, just maybe not as much as they did when they were younger.

I love this quote from Nancy Seither, author of *Empty Nest: Strategies to Help Your Kids Take Flight*, "All of a sudden, the nest is empty. The birds have gone, and what had been a constant blur of activity is now nothing more than a few discarded feathers. Silence mutes all that was colorful, and it is time to reestablish our significant place in an ever-changing world."[4]

How will you reestablish your significant place in an ever-changing world? If you were a stay-at-home parent or even if you are just faced with more freedom now that the kids are growing up, how do you want to show up for the next 20 years?

Whatever the cause, the times in your life when your world is upended can be painful, infused with self-doubt and leave you questioning what's next. These times can also lead to the greatest and most rewarding chapters in your life. In the business mentoring group, I belong to; we refer to those times when life seems so *hard* as being "in the swamp." We are wading through stagnant water with mosquitoes buzzing around our heads, thinking that it's always going to be this way. But if we keep moving, no matter how painful, we will eventually come out into the beautiful forest where the birds are singing, and the sun is shining through the trees. Leveraging the "shake ups" in your life to change people's lives means going from being in the swamp to standing in the lush, green forest.

THE GAME UPPERS

Game uppers are people who already volunteer their time; they show up to galas and sit on boards. They get a rush out of helping others through the organizations they support. The problem is when they go to the galas or board meetings and observe what the founders of organizations and companies are able to do for their communities, they feel a pang of envy. They say to themselves *if she can do that, why can't I? I've got ideas to fix problems in my community. I want to be the one stepping up to make change, not just sitting here eating dessert.*

Beth Bengtson is a great example of this. Beth's career-long desire to connect business with purpose led her to adopt a 1% give back model in her business, Hale Advisors. Since its inception, the firm gives 1% of its revenue to advance women's causes. But that wasn't enough for Beth. Although the check got bigger each year, Beth was frustrated because she knew it would only grow so far and so fast. She wanted to do more. "I realized we need to do more to mentor women and help them recognize their potential," Beth said.[5] She found that only 1.2% of philanthropic giving goes to support women's causes[6] and thought,

45

what if I can direct thousands of businesses to elevate women in the workforce? So, in 2018, she founded Working for Women, "a nonprofit 501(c)3 organization that matches and builds relationships between businesses and non-profit organizations that are working to elevate women to enter and stay in the workforce."[7]

LEGACY CREATORS

Leaving a legacy is a meaningful goal for people, but many of my clients aren't satisfied with simply leaving a legacy of money once they depart this world. They want to take more vivid and tangible actions. They want to feel their legacy. They want to live it.

Take Gary (not his real name), for instance. He built an insurance agency and now wants to give back to the community. In a sense, he feels like he has taken so much from the community, and now it is time to give back. He wants to start a foundation to help issues in his community. His eyes lit up when he read the back of my business card, "Discover your personal path to go from being charitable to being a Changemaker." He said, "That's what I want. To be a Changemaker."

Why do some of us feel such a strong pull to get our legacy in order? Is it a reflection of unfinished business in our lives? Does it stem from a lack of personal fulfillment? Why is legacy important to us? Why does it matter to us what happens after we're dead? And should you feel selfish for thinking about your legacy in the context of giving back to your community?

A legacy is something you hand down to the future. It's the marks you make while you are here and how those marks represent how you showed up in life. It's the imprint you make on your family, your community, your industry and the world.

There is a simple psychological reason for your desire to leave a legacy. Ego. Your sense of self-worth and self-importance pushes you to think beyond your lifetime and imagine how you will be remembered. You can even think of it as a desire for immortality. Knowing that after your death, your imprint on the world will last. It's the belief that your life matters, that is has a point, beyond today.

Legacy combats the fear of future (or current) irrelevance, of the feeling of being or becoming nothing. It's how we make sure we are remembered. It's why people carve their names in trees along hiking trails. To ensure that they're "seen" by those who came after them on the trail. (There are much more positive ways to leave a legacy, by the way).

> *If you embrace your legacy and build your changemaking dream with it in mind, you are more likely to build enduring change because you will think beyond helping one person today. You will think how you can create lasting change that will be recognized for years, if not generations, to come.*

And it's a way to combat the fear of death. Part of our fear of death is that we are afraid to let go of the things we've created in our life. Our relationships, our life's work, what we hold close to our hearts.

Often, it's easier to face death and letting go because we have a sense of fulfillment or completeness. But when we live with regret, with the specter of unfulfilled dreams or ambition, we live in greater fear of death.

That's not to say that even if every item on our bucket list is checked off that we will open our arms and say "Okay, Death. I'm ready." We are biological beings and the fight to survive in order pass on our genetics to the next generation is strong.[8]

Is the desire to leave a legacy selfish? No. Wanting to be recognized and remembered is a human trait. It's natural. If you embrace your legacy and build your changemaking dream with it in mind, you are more likely to build enduring change because you will think beyond helping one person today. You will think how you can create lasting change that will be recognized for years, if not generations, to come.

CRITICAL RESPONDERS

When you, your family or your community are directly impacted by a problem or an event, and you spring into action to protest, counteract or find a solution, you are a Critical Responder.

The reaction and fast action of ordinary people who (unintentionally, in some cases, and intentionally in other cases) became Changemakers, after events like the Pulse Nightclub shooting in 2016, Hurricane Maria in Puerto Rico in 2017 and the Flint, Michigan water crisis (2014-present) epitomize Critical Responders.

In 2018, the world watched and listened as students from Marjory Stoneman Douglas High School stood up in front of cameras and legislators and demanded change after 17 of their classmates and teachers were killed by a gunman while they sat in afternoon classes. Those kids didn't plan to become Changemakers. They didn't take special classes or earn degrees. They were propelled forward into changemaking by their pain, grief and anger.

Critical response doesn't have to follow an act of violence or health crisis. The response since the election of President Donald Trump is another example of critical response. Millions of people have shown up to protest the ban of Muslim citizens from certain countries from entering the United States; efforts to repeal the Affordable Care Act; efforts to prohibit transgender people from serving in the military and the separation of children from their parents at the Mexico-U.S. border.

Erin Chung was a stay-at-home mom who had moved from liberal New York City to Bergen County, New Jersey, a "red-pocket" of New Jersey. She felt like a fish out of water. When Donald Trump first started to run for President, Erin thought, *people won't vote for him.* Erin had been a marketing manager and publicist for the Miss Universe Organization for more than five years and didn't think that voters would relate to him. She was dismayed when she saw signs supporting Donald Trump pop up around her town. She said the morning after the presidential election; she was "devastated but not shocked." She thought she was uniquely positioned to lead a grassroots organization to protest President Trump's policies because she had worked for him. So, she began to organize and joined forces with like-minded people in her community. They hosted their first rally in Wycoff, New Jersey on January 21, 2016, the day of the Women's March in Washington, D.C. They put flyers up around town and ran an ad in the local newspaper. They quickly registered an LLC, so they would be protected legally. Erin said, "Everything [we did] was brand new. None of us had done it before. It was the blind leading the blind." The morning of the rally, Erin told her husband that they had to be prepared that it might just be their core group and families standing in front of the town hall. Her husband said, "That's fine if it's just us." Hundreds of people showed up that day. People kept coming up to her and thanking her for holding the rally, saying things like, "I couldn't go to DC. I couldn't go to New York, but you gave me something I could do locally." An elderly person using a wheelchair said, "I can't get around, but I live in the next town, and I could get here."

18 months later, Erin is running the advocacy organization, Women for Progress and meeting with leaders like U.S. Senator, Cory Booker and former Vice President, Joe Biden. She and her collaborators are organizing protest events against gun violence and immigration policies; they are spearheading letter-writing campaigns and

educational events. "Women for Progress is a network of women whose mission is to raise awareness, educate and connect individuals to activism on a wide range of progressive issues including women's health, gun violence prevention, environmental protection, human rights and equality for all."[9]

Erin didn't set out to launch an organization. She responded to a crisis by taking small actions that grew into a movement.

Repurpose Your Skills

Again, reinventing yourself into a Changemaker doesn't mean you have to start over. Part of reinventing yourself is deciding what skills you want to use going forward. This doesn't necessarily mean you need to develop a whole new set of skills. Trust me; you'll have plenty of opportunities to develop new skills on your Changemaker journey.

Let's first focus on repurposing the skills you already have. Remember Ruth who created a whole new product line and mission using skills she had already mastered?

I often am asked, or rather am told, by women that they would love to have a career with more personal meaning or they would love to start a passion project to help people in their community, but they don't think they have the skills to make a difference.

That's simply not true. If you want to make a difference and you are willing to put in the work that it will take, invest in yourself and ask for help, it doesn't matter what skills you first apply.

First, I can guarantee that almost any skill you have can be used to help someone. And you can combine the skills you already have with the skills you learn, or you can team up with someone who has skills that complement your skills.

Here's an example of a woman who took this very route. Eva Karene Romero is part of my Ordinary, Extraordinary Changemaker Series. She left an unfulfilling career in academia to search for a new path that would allow her to make an impact on her community and the world in a way that made sense to her.

"I dreamed of being a filmmaker, but I never thought that would happen. I didn't have the knowledge. I didn't have the resources. I didn't feel like I had the connections. I was like, 'maybe in some next life, or way in the future; I will be able to take a lot of time or money and put it towards a documentary filmmaking course, workshop or degree.'"

Eva kept pushing forward, despite her doubts. Her vision was to make a film about gender violence in her native country of Paraguay, and she wasn't going to let her inexperience stop her.

She became friends with a Paraguayan film director who was intrigued by gender issues, but he didn't have a handle on the issue or an entry point into the issue of gender violence. Eva knew the issue well. And so, they decided to direct a documentary together.

"I had never directed anything before. I had never worked on a film before. But I definitely have some skills that transferred. I had done mostly research and writing. I knew how to interview somebody, to ask them the right questions, and to dig and find out more about things as they come up."

Eva's film, Kuña, about gender violence in Paraguay, is in production and will be available in the near future.

I have learned that often what you mean when you say you don't have any skills that are needed to give back is that you are so focused on the skills you use every day in your job, that you forget about all the other skills you have. I get it. The thought of using the same skills you use every day to give back can be less than inspiring. But there are lots of exceptions to this rule, and it is possible to use the same skills in a new way or with a new group of people that will give you great satisfaction.

I help my clients identify the strengths and skills they want to use to give back. Not the ones they think they should use, not necessarily the ones they are already using in their current life, but the ones they WANT TO USE.

What's the difference between a strength and a skill? A strength comes naturally to you. A skill is developed or learned (or can be developed or learned). For example, my strength might be that I am witty; whereas, my skill might be that I am a clever improv comedian. My strength might be my sense of adventure; whereas, my skill might be planning life-changing retreats in faraway places.

Naming and owning your strengths and skills will help you design a way to give back that takes advantage of a.) who you are, and b.) the time and effort you have spent gaining particular knowledge in your life. It will also help you understand how you can best hit the ground running and where you need to seek partnerships or other types of help.

Now is your time to dream big. If you are going to spend your time and your resources helping others and becoming a Changemaker, why not do it in a way that is going to leave you feeling happy and fulfilled?

Renew Your Soul

When I say "soul," I am not referring to the word in a religious sense. I mean how you are emotionally connected with your life. How you show up and interact with your own dreams and standards for yourself and the overall sense of alignment you feel with how you are living your life.

One woman I interviewed for my book, a successful wealth manager, told me that giving back to her community in a way that has deep personal meaning allows her to be good at her job. She explained that working in the financial industry "can suck the soul right out of you." You are measured by how much you produce, which inevitably impacts how you interact with your clients and your colleagues, and how you feel about yourself in relation to your work. She looks at her involvement in creating change in her community as soul renewing and as a counterbalance to her career in wealth management.

> *Fast-forward, and it's 20-30 years after graduating high school, and we're asking ourselves, "Okay. I created this career, this family, this life. Now what? What more can I do? How do I align the rest of my life with who I want to be now, at this point in my life?"*

Now, you may not feel like your job is sucking the soul out of you, but there is often a sense of counterbalance that many of my clients seek. I interviewed, Shamini Dhana, Founder of Dhana, Inc., an ethical fashion brand committed to using clothing to better connect people and our planet, for this book. She talked about the strong desire and even the tradition of "giving back" as a symptom of a society that focuses so much on "taking" that giving back becomes a necessary counteraction. Her point was that we shouldn't focus on giving back as a separate function but that we should design our lives so that we are always in balance between taking and giving. While I agree with this wholeheartedly, I don't think a lot of people, including my clients, have spent their lives greedily taking without consideration for other people, animals and our planet. I think that life has a momentum carrying us forward. We go to school, get jobs, build families and buy what we need to care for our families, which means we have to make money to pay the bills. We operate within a system and society that, in some ways, dictates the rules of how we operate. And it's not possible to rewrite the rules every step of the way while simultaneously keeping up with our daily lives. This is why, before we know it, we look up and wonder how our life became misaligned with our values. Fast-forward, and it's 20-30 years after graduating high school, and we're asking ourselves, "Okay. I created this career, this family, this life. Now what? What more can I do? How do I align the rest of my life with who I want to be now, at this point in my life?"

It's important to pay attention to these questions at whatever time of your life they appear, whether it's when you are in your 20s or your 80s. It's not too late, and it's not too early.

You are right on time.

About Guilt

When I speak to groups, someone usually brings up guilt. In one section in the beginning of one of my keynote speeches I ask the audience to raise their hand if they've ever looked outside their car window, seen a problem and then said, "Someone should do something about that." Then I talk about how most people will think of at least three ideas of what *they* could do about the problem. But then they tell themselves, *I don't have time. Who am I to think I can change things?* Or, *someday I will do something...when I have enough money in my 401(k) or my kids are out of the house.* I ask, "And then what happens? Problems in our communities get worse. Kids continue to kill themselves and each other. Our transgender brothers and sisters are denied basic rights. Millions of unwanted dogs and cats are euthanized each year."

At that point, almost every time I give this talk, someone says, "Great. Now I just feel guilty." One woman, who had asked me to come speak to her group, even jumped up and ran to the front of the room when I was done speaking and said, "No matter what you are doing, you are

54

doing your best," in an effort to relieve the guilt anyone might have been feeling.

I'm not trying to make anyone feel guilty. I'm also not judging anyone for taking action or not taking action. It's just that I have seen what happens when people take their idea they have for creating change in their communities and put action behind it. They change lives! They transform our communities, in big and small ways. And, (almost even more importantly), they transform their own lives. They renew their soul. They feel good about the imprint they are making on the world, and about the legacy they are living.

> *Guilt isn't a motivation; it's a symptom of the untapped power you have to create change.*

Becoming a Changemaker is not about relieving your guilt. I don't want you to do this kind of work if the reason that you choose to do it is to relieve your guilt. You probably won't be effective, and you probably won't stick with it. Besides, guilt usually shows up in this context because you haven't taken action on your better-world idea or, if you don't have an idea yet, your desire to be part of finding a solution. In Chapter 4, you'll have a chance to dig into your motivations behind wanting to become a Changemaker but keep this in mind: Guilt isn't a motivation; it's a symptom of the untapped power you have to create change.

When you reinvent yourself into a person who works to create change, whether it's because of your desire to leave a legacy or you are responding to a crisis, you change. You discover new ways of showing up in the world. What this looks like is different for every person. For some, it means going from being a corporate executive who had every minute of her day scheduled, to living and working in a rural town in another country where time has a completely different rhythm and finding great freedom and a renewal of herself within that new concept of time. I changed from someone who was frustrated and depressed because I knew I had more to give, to someone who can't wait to take on the next challenge, to help the next person who sees a problem in her community and is ready to do something about it.

Go Deeper

1. What makes you curious about creating your next act as a Changemaker? Which of the five reasons people reinvent themselves as Changemakers can you relate to? How?

2. What does legacy mean to you? What do you want your legacy to be?

    Workbook Bonus: Legacy Quiz

3. What are your core values? How are your life and career aligned and not aligned with your core values?

4. What skills and strengths do you want to use to bring about the change you want to see?

    Workbook Bonus: Skill Shifter Mini Course

5. How does guilt show up in our life? What are three actions you can take to remedy guilt?

CHAPTER 2:

The Role of Changemaker (Taking It On)

"Changemaker: Anyone who is taking creative action to solve a social problem."
- Ashoka Changemakers

In 2001, Toni Maloney was a successful mid-career marketing executive in New York. She was living a pretty normal life, running her own firm, paying the bills, spending time with her husband, Ray.

Then the planes hit the Twin Towers and the Pentagon, and her perspective shifted. Like most people, she was stunned by what happened on 9/11. She asked herself, *how did we get here? How could this happen? I thought everyone loved us.*

Unlike most people, myself included, Toni wasn't satisfied with simply asking this question. She wanted to play a role in building a more peaceful world so an event like 9/11 would never happen again.

But she didn't know what to do or where to begin. And she didn't know whether she could make a difference. She only knew she needed to try.

Toni began with what she knew best—business—to see what role it could play in peacebuilding.

"I was invited to a conference in Geneva at the UN. It was a conference of 700 women. All but 25 of them were female religious and spiritual leaders. And I was among 25 businesswomen. The businesswomen eventually decamped to the hotel bar for cigarettes and white wine, and said, 'Well praying is good but there must be a faster way.'"

Toni did not know exactly what she was going to do or how she was going to do it, but within a year, she found 60 business women who wanted to join the movement. She started the Business Council for Peace (Bpeace) in 2002. Bpeace spurs economic activity in conflict-affected countries through small and medium-sized businesses to reduce the poverty and desperation that so often seeds violence.

Bpeace's motto is "More Jobs Mean Less Violence."

In the past 15 years, Bpeace has helped companies in countries such as Afghanistan, El Salvador and Guatemala create jobs that have impacted the lives of nearly 21,000 people. Today, Bpeace's portfolio of business creates $81 million in revenue for their communities.

This is Toni's legacy. Never would she have imagined as she sat watching the events of 9/11 unfold, the number of lives she would change because she had an idea and took action on it.

In this chapter, you will learn what a Changemaker is and how you can become one. Together we will go through the three key points that you must have clarity on to start your journey on becoming a Changemaker. I think you will find some surprises in the following pages, so read carefully.

What is a Changemaker?

If you haven't heard of the term "Changemaker" before or aren't familiar with its meaning, you aren't alone. It's a term that is credited to Bill Drayton, Founder of *Ashoka: Everyone a Changemaker,* a program that identifies and supports the world's leading social entrepreneurs. Bill is the founder of the modern social enterprise movement.

Ashoka defines a Changemaker as "…anyone who is taking creative action to solve a social problem." And you have read my definition in an earlier portion of this book: "A Changemaker is somebody who takes action to make change in their community."

I love these examples that Ashoka uses to describe the incredible diversity of Changemakers:

"Changemakers are school children in Haiti creating new traffic safety systems, American truckers preventing human trafficking, and Nobel Peace Prize winners bringing banking to Bangladesh and fighting for child rights in India. They can

come from anywhere in the world; they can come from any sector, and most importantly, they can have any political leaning."[10]

I'll add my own examples of a successful banker who uses her expertise in currency to save hundreds of thousands of dollars for NGOs (nongovernmental organizations—we call them nonprofits in the U.S.), a pair of hard-hitting entrepreneurs who are changing the way women play golf and empowering women and girls as a core part of their business model, and my client, Stephanie, a mom who, after staying home to raise her four girls (including triplets!), is reinventing herself as an advocate for the non-profit sector and is now helping other stay-at-home-moms use their skills and passion to create stronger nonprofits.

Anyone has the potential to be a Changemaker (yes, you!). A Changemaker doesn't have to be someone who sets out to improve an entire system (like the judicial system in the U.S.) or fix a giant problem (like our changing climate). People become Changemakers by taking small actions designed to change the status quo.

Remember the question from the last chapter that I like to ask when I speak to groups? Have you ever looked out your car window, seen a problem in your community and thought, *someone should do something about that?* That's the first step to becoming a Changemaker—recognizing that there is a problem or that an issue could be made better. The second step is recognizing that "someone" is you.

What is the difference between being a Changemaker and someone who simply supports social causes through volunteering, participating in movements or donating goods or money?

Toni Maloney could have simply volunteered for the Red Cross or donated to the families of the victims of the terrorist attacks. But that wasn't enough for her. She wanted to do her part to make sure that

9/11 never happened again. A lofty goal, to be sure, but the point is she took creative action.

A Changemaker identifies a problem and takes action. She uses her skills, ideas, networks and creativity to try to solve the problem. She's not satisfied with adopting an already-tested solution to a problem, say bringing reusable bags to the supermarket, but instead, looks to find a more permanent solution, like creating legislation in her town that bans the distribution of plastic bags in local stores.

A Changemaker isn't satisfied with simply helping. She wants to transform. And she isn't looking for a quick fix to make herself feel like a good person. She's obsessed with the problem and helping to find a solution to that problem.

Laying the Foundation

I hope at this point you are starting to imagine yourself going beyond donating your time and money and that you will take your idea for a better world and put action behind it. (By the way, you don't have to start an organization or company to be a Changemaker. Internal Changemakers, sometimes called social "intrapreneurs" make changes within existing companies and organizations.)

If your heart is racing and you've got butterflies in your stomach just thinking about it, don't worry, that means you are on the right track. As Monica Garrido, Co-Founder and President of One Refugee Child told me when I interviewed her for this book, "If you're not uncomfortable, you aren't pushing yourself hard enough." Monica should know. She's a mother of four and a competitive triathlete.

When people schedule a free discovery call with me, my goal is to give them an opportunity to put their voice to the changemaking idea that has been bouncing around their head and to help them get clarity around how to bring that idea to life. The call also allows me to understand the impact the person wants to have in their community and how ready they are to make it happen. Are they ready to jump in with both feet, test the waters by dipping a toe in, or are they putting up a lot of roadblocks in the form of reasons why they can't make their changemaking idea a reality?

I've found that my most successful clients have clarity on these three key points by the time they launch their journey of becoming a Changemaker:

1. They are ready to reinvent themselves
2. They are ready to clear the time in their life
3. They are ready to invest in themselves and their ideas

REINVENTION

One of the best decisions I made when starting the Women's Changemaker Mentorship™ was to invest in a mastermind group online. After my first meeting with the group, it was as if the clouds had parted and the sun shone down on my idea. I didn't realize how valuable it would be to have other women listen to my idea and give me feedback and validation. I gained the confidence, as well as the support; I needed to move my idea forward. The group also provided a space for me to step into my new identity. I'll never regret the money I spent to join that group.

Reinvention is hard. Reinventing yourself into someone who has the potential to change their community takes your aspiration to a whole different level. It feels bigger. More is at stake. It isn't just about you anymore; it's about the lives that you will change.

I work with a lot of mid-career women. For many of my clients and potential clients, the idea of taking on the new role of Changemaker is both exciting and scary. It's exciting because doing something new and embracing a novel challenge can be rejuvenating and fun. Not only do you get to put your ideas into action; you get to align your interests and goals with your actions to create personal fulfillment, *and* you get to help your community.

For many of my clients (and for me), reinvention can also be scary. The loss of our current identity and the idea of moving away from what is familiar keeps some of us from stepping up to create change in our lives (and the world).

I am not saying that you have to give up your job to create your next act. But, if you do, shifting your identity is something you'll have to consider. Even if you don't leave your job or move gradually into your next act, your identity may shift.

The fear of losing or shifting your identity is very real for many people. The associated stress and paralysis associated can be particularly challenging for women who built their careers in the 1970s through the 1990s.

Let's face it, though; the game was even harder back then when we jumped into our careers than it is today. Women have fought fiercely to build businesses and climb the corporate ladder to achieve positions of power and success. This is true whether you are the CEO of a Fortune 500 company or a tenured professor at a local community college. You earned your title(s), and your identity that goes along with that title. Giving that up to take on a new challenge can be disorienting, to say the least.

I talked about my journey around identity in the Introduction. In some ways, I am still finding my new identity. As the saying goes, "It is about the journey, not the destination." With every new client and every new program I design, and especially as it pertains to writing this book, I see more clearly the movement of change agents I am creating. I step more strongly into my new reality and identity. I have to admit that it was pretty scary at first and I am forever grateful for my clients who, unwittingly, have helped me find my path of reinvention.

One mistake that I made when I first started out on my reinvention journey was to try to do it on my own. I didn't realize all the different decisions I would have to make, and I certainly didn't realize how many options were out there. I also didn't realize how lonely it could be to try to create something without cocreators. I kissed a few frogs (aka identities) before I found my princess (aka the Women's Changemaker Mentorship™).

When I first left my staff position, I was scared and immediately fell into fundraising consulting. This was a good move in the sense that I had income coming in, but I wasn't excited about it, and it took my time and energy away from doing what I really wanted to do—help women use their skills, ideas and power to make positive change in their communities.

I also got distracted by a mission I am very passionate about, but this wasn't, as I learned, something I felt prepared to move forward. I am a big fan of *The Moth*, (a non-profit group based in New York City dedicated to the art and craft of storytelling) and had been telling people's stories through my fundraising work for years. So, I launched a company called *StoriedGlobal* with the intention to help organizations and individuals tell their stories. To make a long story short, I realized that although I love helping people tell their personal stories, working with organizations quickly became more about fundraising than capturing stories. I had left a career in fundraising and knew I needed some distance from it.

I also realized that the learning curve was very steep. While I had some experience and natural talent in helping people tell their personal stories, there were a lot of skills (video, editing, technology) that I would have to learn before I could become competitive in the marketplace. I *love* to learn new things, but for me, it wasn't the right choice to spend tons of time gaining new skills to do something that I wasn't convinced I wanted to turn into a business. And I had this pull to help people help more people! Then suddenly, it was as if the universe sent me a sign because to get *StoriedGlobal* started; I took on a pro bono project for a non-profit in Connecticut. (Looking back, this is telling because I realized I wasn't confident enough in my skills to ask for payment, and so I was willing to give my time and ideas away for free!) The night before I was to lead my first workshop for the organization, I came down with a horrible stomach bug. The thought of getting out of bed was impossible, let alone showing up to facilitate a workshop for 30 high school students. The stomach bug passed after a few hours, but the executive director of the organization never returned my calls.

I put that idea on the back burner and moved forward with creating the Women's Changemaker Mentorship™. Recently I realized, through writing and interviewing people for this book, that I still wanted to help people tell their stories, just not in the way I had originally thought. Part of the changemaking methodology that I created and use with my clients involves using your own story to influence action. So, I am launching a publishing company for my clients and others who want to tell their stories of their journey to create change. Now, they will have a place where like-minded people can help put their story out into the world. And, I'm calling the company, StoriedGlobal. It's funny how ideas have a way of circling around to reappear in your life.

CLEARING THE TIME

When I ask people what keeps them from implementing the ideas they have for creating change in their community, one of the most common reasons I hear that holds them back is time. Here's the truth. You can design your changemaking initiative the way you want. You can quit your job and put all your time into it. You can start small and gradually increase your time until you reach a tipping point when you are ready to dedicate more of your time, or you can design a passion project that fits within the other elements of your life (job, family, etc.).

My friend Awa lives in Dakar, Senegal. She works a full-time government job. Once or twice a year, my wife and I get a message from Awa saying she's going to be in town and wants to see us. Her reason for coming to New York City a couple of times a year has nothing to do with her job or even a vacation. You see, several years ago Awa's brother was tragically killed in an automobile accident. Since then, Awa has dedicated her free time to promoting road safety in her country and around the world. She founded LASER International, an organization that collaborates with the United Nations and non-governmental organizations around the world to promote road safety and road traffic injury prevention. She comes to New York to meet with collaborators at the United Nations.

For your dream, It might make sense to start by writing a book, doing a photography project or just hosting conversations around the issues that are important to you. Most of my clients build out their idea and get more clarity before they commit to it full-time. In recognizing this need, I have built my program to give my clients space to start and progress at their own speed. Some of my clients move very quickly toward their goals, some more slowly.

INVESTING IN YOURSELF

Let's face it; unless you are wealthy or have wealthy, generous friends, money is always going to be an obstacle in pretty much anything we do in life. These three standards are essential when thinking about your next act.

- You must invest in yourself and your ideas to succeed
- You can do good *and* make money
- People want to support your ideas

<u>Invest in yourself and your ideas</u>

If you were a venture capitalist, would you invest in your own ideas? When I ask my clients this, after giving the question some thought, the majority answer yes. I then ask them why they are good investments. They tell me it's because their ideas are backed by experience. They can keep a track record of their success as they value their inspiration and their unstoppable belief in the change they seek to make in the world.

The truth is that if you are serious about becoming a Changemaker, you will have to invest in yourself and your ideas. I'm not saying you will need to empty your 401(k) but you will have to invest both money and time if you are going to put action behind your ideas to create the impact you want to make.

What if you had planned financially for your reinvention? In the same way that we save for our kids' college, retirement or buying our first home, we should have a "reinvention fund" we contribute to a little each month from the time we start working. It doesn't have to be a big contribution. If you put in an average of $150 a month for 20 years, over the course of your career (your "first act"), you'll have at least $36,000-$40,000 to pad your reinvention. That's not a huge amount, but it does give you the freedom to explore the possibilities of your next act, at least for a few months. And if you don't need this kitty for your reinvention, you can use it for something else.

If you've already reached the reinvention point in your life, consider taking part of your savings and calling it your reinvention fund. Label and own your investment in your next act. You are worth it. Your legacy is worth the investment.

Doing Good *and* Making Money

There is no law that says to create positive change you have to take a vow of poverty. There are a growing number of examples of social enterprises, B Corporations and small businesses that are generating profits and collaborating with stakeholders in their communities to make powerful social, environmental and economic change.

Two of my clients, Tami Fujii and Dianne Celuch, founded Kinona Sport, a women's golf apparel company. Avid golfers, the idea for their company grew out of a recognition that women didn't have a lot of good choices for fashionable, comfortable golf clothes. So, they set out to design a line of golf apparel that is flattering for any woman. As they say on their website, "Because no matter her shape or size, every woman deserves to feel great doing what she loves."

When I worked with Tami and Dianne, I quickly realized their business, and their passion, isn't just about golf clothes; it's about getting more women on the golf course, where business deals happen. They describe their business as a three-legged stool. The first leg is giving women something functional and flattering to wear on and off the golf course. The second is creating a community of women around golf and giving women the opportunity to start second careers. They do this through their "Champions Program" where "women can invest in a 'kit' and host shopping parties at their home, office, or at a club."[11] The third leg is what Dianne and Tami hired me to help them with: giving back to the community. They wanted to pick a community partner, a non-profit, that could help them fulfill their dream of running a business that is also creating change in the community. In our Strategy Session, I asked them to dig into what they stood for, what was important to them and how they wanted to show up in their communities, both as individuals and as a company. I helped them see that what they had in common was a desire to make an impact at the community level and to play a part in mentoring girls. So, they explored give back opportunities that allowed them to do that. We also talked about what it means to be in partnership with a non-profit organization and how important it is for everyone involved that it is a relationship of reciprocity and collaboration and not one where they are simply writing a check to an organization every month. They have since partnered with The First Tee, a national organization that teaches kids values through golf.

People Want to Support Your Ideas

One of the biggest blocks many of my clients have concerns fundraising and how they will make the money to support their idea, whether it's philanthropy or investment they need. They don't want to ask people for money. Although not easy, fundraising is not as scary as you think. It can actually be extremely life-affirming. If you invest in yourself and your ideas, if you take the time and get the help you need to build out your idea, to demonstrate how you are going to make change, whether it's through a for-profit business, a non-profit or a foundation, people will invest in you and your idea.

Go Deeper

1. Using the definition of Changemaker, can you identify people in your community who are Changemakers? What change are they making? How did they get started?

2. If money were no object, what would reinventing yourself look like? What would you spend your days doing? How much time would you dedicate to your new self?

3. What concerns and challenges do you have about your reinvention? What support and help do you need to overcome those concerns and challenges?

4. When was a time in your life when you invested in yourself and your ideas? What was the result? How did that make you feel?

5. If you were a venture capitalist with $100,000 to invest in a person, would you invest in yourself? Why?

PART 2:

The Art of Changemaking

CHAPTER 3:

Changemaking as a Way of Life

*"Issue: a subject or problem that people are
thinking and talking about."*
-Cambridge Dictionary

Last year, I was introduced through email to Dianne Grossman, founder of Mallory's Army™ Foundation. Dianne's 12-year-old daughter was bullied so badly she had taken her own life the previous summer. Twelve. Years. Old. Timidly, I reached out to Dianne, to see if I could help in some way. In Dianne's response to my email, she told me that they were looking for a CEO, someone with startup experience and had a roadmap to success. Then, she included a line that really brought home to me what she must be going through—not only as a mother who had lost her child, but as a woman who had been thrust into taking action by the most personal type of tragedy imaginable, "As you can imagine, passion or the want/desire is not what I lack, nor do we lack the time/attention. This is a dream handed to us, not one we asked for."

Some people set out to change the world, for humanitarian reasons, as a challenge, or both. Some seek deeper meaning in their lives and look for it in the service of others. Some are thrust into changemaking because of personal tragedy, like Mallory's mom, Dianne.

There is no one way to go about making change. Changemakers confront social problems from varying perspectives, backgrounds, skill sets, resources and motivations.

In Chapter 2, I talked about what it means to step into your role as Changemaker. In this chapter, I'll talk about what's often involved in the art of changemaking. I'll address how you narrow in on the issue you want to focus on, give you six common types of Changemakers and explain what it means to be a social "intrapreneur." Finally, we'll talk about starting with your own community.

Pick Your Issue

I'm going to give you a glimpse into how my brain works when it comes to problems in our communities.

7:00 am - I listen to a podcast about the crisis in the criminal justice system in the U.S. and think, *I'm going to do something about this.*

9:15 am - I read a blog post about how women need to run for office at the local level and think, *maybe I should run for office?*

11:30 am - I see a GoFundMe Campaign to help a dog who needs life-saving surgery, so I pull out my credit card and donate $10.

2:00 pm - I get an email from a student exchange program saying they desperately need volunteers to help run their initiative this year. I consider volunteering.

3:30 pm - My friend on Facebook posts a passionate plea to join her in protesting against the Immigration and Customs Enforcement (ICE) raids happening in our state. I think, *count me in!*

5:30 pm - I hear a story on NPR about the opportunities to invest in female-led startups and think, *I'm going to talk to my wife tonight about starting a venture capital fund.*

7:00 pm - I go to the supermarket, buy five items and the checkout clerk puts them in three separate plastic bags before I remember to give him my reusable bag. This infuriates me because I HATE the way we consume plastic bags like they are made out of disappearing ink. (Note: they take 10-1000 years to decompose.) I leave determined to do something about plastic bag use in our town.

8:00 pm - I sit on the couch and watch *Million Dollar Listing* so I can stop the spin in my head from all the issues I should be doing something about.

We are surrounded by people talking about important topics or problems—our friends, families and colleagues, on social media, in the news, etc. One of the effects of having such an intense level of access to news and media all the time is that we are bombarded by information about problems in our communities and world. It's emotionally, mentally and sometimes physically exhausting. It feels like you're on one of those rides at an amusement park that whips you around in different directions, leaving you confused and disoriented. I call this feeling of being so overwhelmed by all the problems in the world that you do nothing and tune it all out, "issue paralysis." The problem is that when we tune out, we feel uninformed and risk not having our voice heard on issues that we care about and that impact our lives.

> *"Take up one idea. Make that one idea your life— think of it, dream of it, live on that idea. Let the brain, muscles, nerves, every part of your body, be full of that idea, and just leave every other idea alone. This is the way to success."*[12]

My cure for "issue paralysis" is to give myself, and my clients, permission to pick one or two issues, put our energy and attention there, and let all the other issues play out in the background.

Although it may seem like you will create a lot of positive impact if you spread yourself across many different causes, there is real benefit to narrowing your focus and going deep on one issue. In her book, *Radical Transformation Leadership*, Monica Sharma introduced me to this quote by Swami Vivekananda, an Indian Hindu monk who lived in the second half of the 19th Century: "Take up one idea. Make that one idea your life—think of it, dream of it, live on that idea. Let the brain, muscles, nerves, every part of your body, be full of that idea, and just leave every other idea alone. This is the way to success."[12]

When I first started my business, I targeted anybody and everybody who was interested in learning more about social issues and getting engaged with them. In fact, the first name of my program was *Engage*. I worked with people who wanted to volunteer, protest, become advocates, who wanted to learn to be better philanthropists, to work for nonprofits and to start new social change initiatives. I also worked with organizations that wanted to create even more impact in their communities. It was exhausting. Because I always give 150% to my clients, I felt like I had to be an expert in all those areas, which meant hours of reading and listening to podcasts, trying to keep up on the latest developments in politics and social change work. I still do a lot of reading and podcast listening, but I've learned to align where I want to spend my energy with what I am trying to accomplish.

I took a step back and looked at what I really enjoyed doing, what I was good at and where I could make the most impact. I quickly realized that there were lots of organizations that match people with volunteer opportunities and teach people to be advocates. There were also programs that helped students and young entrepreneurs become social change agents. But what I heard over and over again from my clients and women who did discovery calls with me was that they were mid-career, wanted to transition to impact-focused work, were interested in starting their own business or organization and felt as though there were few resources to help them. So, I narrowed my focus to work with mid-career professional women who wanted to use their skills, ideas and passion to become Changemakers in their communities. Sure, I sometimes work with people who fall outside that category, but I'm careful to keep my attention focused on my dream of creating a movement of women Changemakers.

But which issue do you choose to focus on? I'll give you a hint. It's not necessarily the issue trending on Facebook. Nor is it the one that everyone in the PTA is supporting. The issue you should focus on is the one that grabs you in a deep, personal embrace. I advise my clients to choose the issue that either makes them boil with anger, cry with grief or bubble over with excitement.

Choose the Type of Changemaker You Want to Be

Often, people call me after they have already started a non-profit organization but don't know how to move it forward. Starting a non-profit, or at least doing the legal registration, as the first step in creating change in your community is a common thing to do. But launching and leading a non-profit organization is not for everyone and isn't the only way to be a Changemaker. One of the key points I advise my clients on is figuring out how they should fit into solving the problem they have identified. This requires taking stock of your skills, what's already being done and deciding where you can create the most impact.

Pulling from hundreds of Changemakers, Ashoka has identified six common types of Changemakers.

Social Architects

Just like architects who design buildings, create new physical structures and improve existing ones, social architects create new social structures in the form of policies, programs, technology and movements (or they alter existing ones) to change human behavior and in turn solve social problems. Within the new or altered social structures, social architects redefine roles and how resources are used and allocated. In today's world, we often call social architects, "disrupters."

Salman Khan, founder of Khan Academy, and Wendy Kopp, Founder of Teach for America and Teach for All, are social architects who have created new ways in which society educates its children (and adults), greatly expanding access to education and improving the quality of education in underserved communities around the world.

Influencers

Influencers use learning and decision making as their mediums to create change. Their goal is to influence how people think and make decisions about a particular issue or set of issues. They use tools like films, articles, blogs, videos, conferences and classes to create a change in mindset and behavior.

In 2011, I worked with two influential thought leaders, Joy Anderson and Jackie VanderBrug at the Connecticut-based Criterion Institute, "a non-profit think tank that works with social change-makers to demystify finance and broaden their perspective on how to engage with and shift financial systems."[13] One of the key initiatives that we worked on was Gender Lens Investing, a movement that promotes investment strategies focused on creating a financial return while also benefiting women. The idea was (and still is, although it has evolved since then) to create more investment capital going into women-owned businesses, companies that employed women and produced goods and services that benefited women and girls. Criterion Institute's role was to convene influencers and engage them in dialogue around the issue to promote and advance Gender Lens Investing on a global level.

Skills Catalyzers

Skills catalyzers focus on the use of expertise and skills to influence change. In short, they figure out how to put human resources to work to create social impact.

My client, Stephanie, who I mentioned before, is creating a program for stay-at-home moms who want to re-enter the workforce via the nonprofit sector, but who need to first gain experience and brush up on their skills to put their expertise, time and ideas to work in the non-profit sector. Stephanie is designing her program to not only help women who have been out of the workforce relaunch themselves but also to provide a pipeline of talent to the Boston non-profit sector area.

Investors

Investors use money and support to bring about change. Philanthropy or donations are no longer the only way to use your money for changemaking. Impact investing is a great example of how money can be used to create better communities.

Veris Wealth Partners is a U.S.-based wealth management firm that helps investors, with a special emphasis on women investors, generate financial returns and reach their impact-investing objectives. Veris helps their clients invest their money in issue areas like climate change and the environment, women and girls, community wealth building, sustainable agriculture and food systems and sustainability and mindfulness.[14]

Inventors

Inventors use technology and tools to create social change. An increasing number of universities have programs that encourage students to invent products to solve sticky social problems.

Here's an example of how one woman put her idea to work to bring clean water to communities. While studying for her PhD in Chemistry at McGill University, Teri Dankovich invented the very first paper-based antimicrobial water filter. Folia Filters™ work similarly to a coffee filter but kill bacteria and can be used anywhere in the world to make safe drinking water. Spoken with a true inventor's spirit, Teri told me, "I think the best advice I can give to someone with an idea is to go and try it. Even if it's not going to be perfect at first, that doesn't really matter. You're going to learn something about what you're trying to do, and you can make it better from what you learn."

Connectors

Connectors build relationships between people and groups of people to bring about change. They unite people through a specific issue or problem sometimes in a particular space, like at a conference, or online through a Facebook or LinkedIn group. If you've noticed someone working to organize you and your neighbors to make change happen in your community, you've witnessed a connector Changemaker at work.

Erin Chung, Founder of Women for Progress, whom I talked about in Chapter 1, is a great example of a connector Changemaker.

Now, maybe you are thinking that you would love to play a part in creating better communities, but you like working within a big corporation. My wife and I have this conversation all the time. I love being an entrepreneur and I was miserable when, decades ago, I worked in a big corporation. On the other hand, she likes working for a big company and thrives within a larger, more complicated system.

Not everyone needs to start a business or organization to play an important part in moving the needle on social and environmental problems. The idea that you have to stop what you are doing in your current career to focus on changemaking is what holds a lot of people back from doing anything at all. (Remember my story about "someday...")?

I will talk more about how you can figure out your role in changemaking in Chapter 5, but I wanted to take a moment to discuss the power of "social intrapreneurs," people who work to fix problems within a company, organization or structure.

Take a look at The Dove Self Esteem Project[15]. The person or team of people who came up with the concept are social intrapreneurs. They are working within the company to change the way the media portrays the bodies of women and girls. They didn't leave their corporation to start a new organization or company; they focused on what they could do to impact the most lives from within Unilever, the company that owns the Dove brand.

Start with Your Community

A lot of us want to help the "less fortunate." We hear stories of problems in other communities and countries and want to alleviate the issues. It's human to want to help and often it's easier or more interesting to focus on problems outside our own community instead of seeing the problems next door. The drawback with this approach is that it's hard to find a viable solution to a problem if you don't understand the problem and the context in which it lives.

Can you imagine if someone walked into your home uninvited and after being there for 10 minutes started naming all the problems you needed to fix in your house and family and then told you how you should fix the problems? It would be annoying, if not infuriating, right? History is filled with examples of people trying to fix problems that they don't understand. I, for one, am guilty of this. I went to Afghanistan wanting to help women without knowing anything about the culture or the real problems of the women I hoped to help. I jumped in without taking enough time to learn and to find the right stakeholders as collaborators. The result was the impact of the project I worked on was limited and short-lived, especially in comparison with many Afghan-led businesses and programs.

I advise my clients to start on their changemaking journey within their own community. Community has a different meaning for each person. It can mean the street you live on, the origin country of your parents or where you visit every summer. Your community can be measured geographically, or it can be a group of people spread across the world. The point is to begin where you at least have a starting knowledge of and connection to the culture, context and problems. That's not to say if you start in your community that you don't have to learn thoroughly about the issue you are trying to address. Communities are complex, and many of us operate within the part of our community where we feel most comfortable and connected.

My friend, Lori Garcia-McCammon, Founder of the True Ridge Foundation, is a passionate advocate for the rights and protection of immigrant women who are victims and survivors of domestic violence. She has such power in her voice and actions that she could easily stand on a national or international stage and call for change, and I won't be surprised when I see her doing just that in the near future. But when Lori, through her job as a social worker in the Hendersonville, North Carolina area, saw that immigrant women living and working in her community—most of them from Mexico and Central America— needed help getting away from domestic violence, she looked closely at what they needed, what was already being provided by other organizations and where there was a gap that she could fill. It was difficult for Lori to know exactly where to begin but she knew she wanted to start with helping the women in her immediate community. Because she lived and worked in Hendersonville, she was able to quickly understand what was needed and was able to start helping women right away. Then in 2018, when U.S. Immigration and Customs Enforcement (ICE) carried out raids in Hendersonville, she was so well plugged into the immigrant community that she was able to quickly respond to help people who were terrified by the raids, many of whom who were afraid to come out of their homes even to buy food for their families. Lori and her team were able to provide resources and services to people who were very distrustful of outsiders because she was known in the immigrant community. The need for True Ridge Foundation's services has grown so much and so quickly that Lori and her team now struggle with how to strategically allocate their time and resources to help the most people. One of the ways that Lori is getting help with this challenge is through my Next Act, Give Back Bootcamp, a two-day transformative workshop that helps people take their ideas and organizations to the next level.

Go Deeper

1. What issue(s) are the most important to you? Why?

   Workbook Bonus: Issue Mapper

2. What type(s) of Changemaker are you or would you like to be?
3. How do you define community in your life? What communities do you belong to?

CHAPTER 4:

Your Inspired Action

"Action: The fact or process of doing something,
typically to achieve an aim."
- Oxford Living Dictionaries

I'm inspired every day by stories of people who have put their creativity to work to find solutions to problems in their communities. From artists like Beyonce and Jay-Z who through their music start global conversations about race and gender, to Sandra Musujusu, a university student in Sierra Leone who is working to develop a cure for a type of breast cancer that is common in women with African ancestry.

When I speak to groups, I ask the questions: "If you could create any legacy you wanted to help leave your community better than when you entered it, what would your legacy look like? What change would you make?" I ask the group to write their answer on a sticky note and put it up on the wall (I call it the "Legacy Wall"), so everyone can see the collection of powerful legacies. Rarely, in all the groups I've spoken to, does someone *not* put something up on the wall. Most people have a vision for what healthier, safer and more just communities look like.

Before I end my talk, I tell the group, "Don't forget your legacy. Make sure you take your idea with you and put it on your refrigerator, so it doesn't slip your mind." Nine out of 10 people leave their sticky note on the wall and go home. Maybe they have been thinking about their idea for so long that they don't need the note, or maybe they aren't ready or don't think they can make their legacy come alive.

Whatever the reason, although most of us have a vision for a better community, a lot of us will probably never do anything to make that vision a reality.

I get it. We live busy lives, and if we think too much about the problems, we just feel guilty because we can't do anything about them. Right? Wrong. Remember, guilt is caused from inaction. Action is a great reliever of guilt. Even taking one small action lessens guilt and can change a life.

I've been talking to people for over two decades about their ideas for creating change. I've also had the great privilege to work with dedicated, committed Changemakers who have worked tirelessly to solve some of our society's biggest problems. People like Dr. Jordan Kassalow, founder of VisionSpring and the EYElliance, who wants every person on this planet to have access to the eyeglasses they need to live a productive life. Then there's Claire Brett Smith, President Emeritus of Aid to Artisans, who had the vision of extending market opportunities to low-income artisans around the world, so they could build profitable businesses and care for their families.

Whether you are someone with an idea you haven't acted on (yet) or you are like Jordan and Claire, who have already changed the lives of millions of people, you have one thing in common with other Changemakers. Vision.

If I were standing in front of you right now, and I handed you a sticky note and asked you to write the change you would make in the world on it, what would you write? Would you have a hard time just picking one thing?

In this chapter, you will learn the importance of understanding your vision for your community and how you can use that as your North Star. You'll also dig deep into your motivation for wanting to create your next act as a Changemaker.

Claim Your Vision

I first met Desiree Adaway when, several years ago, I sought her help as a coach to help me find clarity about my career path during the unhappy period of my life that I talked about in the Introduction of this book. I have always been inspired by her singular, concrete vision for what she wants our world to look like. Today, Desiree is a trainer, coach and speaker focused on equity and inclusion. She works with organizations and businesses to help them determine in what ways their company culture is inclusive and in what ways it is exclusive. Her vision is to destroy oppressive systems and create liberation for *all* people. She stands for community, connection and the understanding that we don't get to leave other people behind. As Desiree says, "We all get free together. None of us get to be left behind. I push back on the idea that we have to know each other in order for me to give you your humanity. I don't have to know you to say you deserve the right to health care, healthy food, clean air, to marry who you want to marry. I don't have to know you personally to know that you deserve that."

I have watched as Desiree's work to promote her vision has evolved over the past few years. In 2015, she wrote a two-line love letter to the sisterhood on Facebook using "Dear Sister" as her greeting. She has written a Dear Sister (not just cister) post every day since. Today, she sends out these powerful posts to 20,000 followers on Facebook and Twitter. She also co-facilitates a course called "Diversity is an Asset" "…that help[s] you develop specific ways to champion diversity, equity, and inclusion work within your organization or business on interpersonal and systemic levels."

Desiree is a compelling example of why It is important to be clear about your vision for the change you want to make in your community (or the world) before you design how you will make it happen. That's not to say it can't or won't change and there isn't a right or wrong way to settle on your vision, but like most things in life, it's helpful to have an idea of where you are headed.

Vision is big picture. It's what you want ultimately to make happen. It's both the change you want to make in the world and the change you want to make in your life by working to make that change. For example, your vision may be that you want to end gun violence in your city and you want to be known as the person who stood up to make that happen.

Your vision can be small in scope. You might be able to accomplish it within a shorter timeframe, or it can be big, and it might take years to complete. It could even reflect your life's work.

Desiree Adaway didn't know how her work was going to unfold (or how it will continue to unfold) when she first started working toward her vision, but she is unwavering in how she wants our communities to look and act and fights tirelessly to make her vision a reality.

Own Your Motivation

My client, Sarah Foster, is the Founder of Stem Like a Girl, an organization in the San Francisco area that "...believe[s] all girls can become scientists and engineers when given the right tools early on to develop their own STEM identity." While leading an engineering project in her son's elementary school class, Sara noticed that fewer girls raised their hands and jumped in to participate. She was struck by the gender gap in participation on a science and math-based activity at such a young age.[16] When I worked with Sarah to help her get clarity about the next steps to launch STEM Like a Girl, she told me that part of her motivation for starting the organization was because when she was a young girl and interested in math and science, she felt alone and not particularly encouraged to pursue her interests. She had carried that feeling with her as she grew up, got her chemical engineering undergraduate degree and biomedical engineering graduate degree, and as she went to work as an engineer in the biotech field. So, when she saw the girls in her son's classroom holding back from participating, she recognized her younger self in those girls. That experience played a big part in her motivation to start STEM Like a Girl.

It's helpful to understand our motivation behind what we do in life. Why do we want to eat healthy? Some of us want to be thin. Others want to have more energy. Still, others, make changes because our loved ones ask us to. Our desire to make a difference is no different.

Often in my first conversation with people about why they want to give back, they tell me something like this: "I want to help people. It doesn't matter what I get out of it as long as I help people." To that, I say, "What a shame! And by the way, I don't believe you." That usually leads to a few uncomfortable moments of silence. Then I explain that I don't believe in altruism. I mean, I believe in the concept. It is lovely, after all. But I don't think it is a practical approach to changing communities. Here's why. When you see a problem in your community that you want to fix, if you go into it thinking, *it doesn't matter what I get out of it as long as I help people*, you are less likely to make transformative change. On the other hand, if you are honest with yourself about your motivations for giving back (which aren't always obvious by the way) and what changes you want to make in your own life and career, and you design a business or organization with your motivations in mind, you are more likely to stick with it and make the transformative change.

I've invented the word "Altruself" to describe how you can be concerned for the well-being of others and also look out for your own dreams, goals and desires. Although this desire is noble, altruism is generally not a big enough motivator to keep most of us interested in changemaking endeavors over the long term. Understanding the WHY behind your desire to get involved in the issues that you care about will help you design a way to make a difference that will be fulfilling to you, and this will cause even more transformation in the lives of others.

People tell me "how rewarding my work must be." They have no idea. But it's not rewarding in the way they mean. They think it's rewarding because I'm "helping people." I've never been comfortable with that assumption. It's not that I don't want to help people. I do. I just can't claim that reason as my primary motivator for choosing the jobs I have.

And I feel inauthentic when the "helping people" label is applied as the headline.

Motivation is a tricky subject, especially when it comes to giving back. There are a lot of resources out there that suggest you should focus on what you give and expect nothing in return. "Give selflessly and be satisfied with the joy you get from helping others," we've all heard that recommendation. There's only one problem with that. You are human. And for most of us, there needs to be a balance between what we give others and what we get in return, especially if we are going to stick with something in the longer term. The balance is different for everyone, but for most people it falls somewhere in between Mother Teresa, as an example of a purer form of altruism, and Ayn Rand, who promoted the concept that each person "exists for his own sake, and the achievement of his own happiness is his highest moral purpose." This is why often altruism is generally not a big enough motivator to keep most of us interested in changemaking over the long term.

You wouldn't choose a career or a hobby without thinking about what you would get out of it, so why would you choose a way to give back without thinking about what you are going to get out of it? Understanding the WHY behind your desire to get involved in the issues that you care about will help you design a way to make a difference that will be fulfilling.

It's not "selfish" to think this way. It's actually the opposite. It shows that you care about making a lasting impact and that you aren't going to be in it for a week or two and then move on to your next "cause."

Joan Shifrin and Catherine Shimony founded Global Goods Partners (GGP) in 2005. Global Goods Partners provides sustainable market access to handcrafted, Fair Trade products through their online store and through wholesale sales to stores around the U.S. and abroad. Their beautiful products are made by women artisans around the world. I met Catherine when they were starting GGP. I have watched them grow their organization into a powerhouse that has touched the lives of more than 20,000 women artisans. One of Joan and Catherine's biggest challenges is maintaining and growing their market share in the online world of retail. "In online retail, it's hard to distinguish between a group that has little connection to communities, and a group like us, who has been doing it for 12 years and established close relationships with communities and artisans." They have seen a lot of startup companies enter and leave the marketplace *and* the artisan communities. Well-meaning people go to a community, fall in love with the handcrafts and want to do something to help artisans. So, they set up a business and make big promises to the artisans about how they are going to sell a lot of their products. But the reality is that sourcing quality products and selling them in a competitive marketplace is not easy. Many people quit when they don't have immediate success or are not getting out of the business what they had hoped, both in terms of personal fulfillment and profit. This is disappointing to the entrepreneur, for sure, but it can be devastating to the artisans who were counting on sales of their products to support their families.

Whether your goal is to give back through your career, a passion project or philanthropy, being honest with yourself about what you want to get in return should be one of your first steps in developing your plan to give back. Put judgment aside and dig deep into your thoughts and feelings on what your reasons are for wanting to give back and become a Changemaker.

I recommend exploring six motivation classifications to dive deeper into your altruistic desires. You might not feel a motivation in each category but be honest with yourself. And you don't have to share this with anyone if you don't want to (if it helps you stay honest). The categories[17] are:

- Incentive
- Fear
- Achievement
- Growth
- Power
- Social

INCENTIVE

Think about incentives as rewards for your changemaking work. Incentives can be monetary or non-monetary and may include salary, tax deductions, benefits and profit (from a for-profit initiative). Non-monetary incentives might include a promotion, a title or a more well-rounded resume.

For three years, I served on the board of directors of Dining for Women, a U.S.-based organization that raises millions of dollars to support women's and girls' causes around the world. Dining for Women is one of the largest giving circles globally and has transformed the way giving circles serve their members by adding quality educational material to philanthropy and community. A giving circle is a group of people who come together to pool their philanthropy to support social causes.

I was very much aligned with the mission of Dining for Women, and I loved the people involved in the organization. But the number one reason I joined the board, given my very busy work schedule, was that I wanted the experience of working in governance in an organization that I knew was an innovator in its space. I received the experience and was able to give my viewpoint and experience to help the organization grow. That's a win-win, in my opinion.

FEAR

Fear can be a big motivator, too. Look at how the Black Lives Matter movement started and gained incredible momentum. Mothers, fathers, grandparents, sisters, brothers, friends and neighbors were fed up seeing their African American loved ones abused and killed by law enforcement, without consequence for law enforcement. People of color are afraid for the lives of their children in their own communities.

Are you motivated to make change because you are afraid of injustices happening or getting worse in your community?

Sometimes fear is very obvious, and sometimes it sits below the service. Sometimes fear is related to a deep-rooted social problem, as is the case with Black Lives Matter. But it can also be your very personal fear of becoming irrelevant in your career and life or fear that you are not using your voice to do something about the problems you see outside of your car window.

My client who wants to start a foundation is afraid that he will be remembered as a guy who only cared about making money. He's spent his entire adult life building successful financial businesses. He's proud of his work and his accomplishments. But he also believes it is his time to give back, and he is afraid he will not have accomplished all that he wants to accomplish in life if he doesn't find a way to complete his legacy.

The fear of not being who you want to be is very real for a lot of people. Unfortunately, fear can also be paralyzing because the fear represents something so important that it's hard to move forward with a plan to get past your fear. You keep putting off your plans, saying you are too busy or that next year will be *the year*. Before you know it, 10 years go by and then you are living with a looming compulsion worse than fear: regret. This will be the regret that you didn't take action 10 years ago when you had the chance.

ACHIEVEMENT

What do you dream of achieving in your next act as a Changemaker? Are you seeking to accomplish a goal or tackle a new challenge while making a difference? Achievement can be general—you want to spur change that feels greater and more meaningful, than what you do in your job every day, or achievement can be specific—you want to publish a book that will help people.

When I first started working with my client, Stephanie, she went back and forth on whether she should start her own consulting business or get a job with an existing organization. As I mentioned earlier, her vision is to help stay-at-home moms going back into the workforce use their talents to strengthen non-profits in the Boston area. When we dug into the question, whether to jump on someone else's train or build her own, she kept coming back to her vision of creating her own company. (Stephanie Lawrence Initiatives). And even though it is still scary as hell sometimes, she knows she really wants to at least try to build her own company, so she can say, "Look what I achieved."

GROWTH

Gail Sheehy, author, journalist and lecturer, once said, *"If we don't change, we don't grow. If we don't grow, we aren't really living."*

The desire for self-improvement, learning and change can be an important motivator for reinventing yourself and for pushing yourself forward toward your better-world idea. And there is probably no better way to experience deep personal growth than to get on the path of trying to create change in the world.

I could write an entire book on the ways I've grown through my work. I think most of the career decisions I've made were motivated by an opportunity to grow. Growth is a big motivator for me.

When I was 23 and living in a Spanish-speaking part of Brooklyn, I hated it when I would walk down the street and couldn't understand what people were saying. I wanted to speak Spanish so badly! So, I sought out an opportunity to move to Costa Rica to work in the Costa Rican office of the student exchange program that I happened to be working for in New York. Actually, I gave up a pretty good job in New York to move! My primary goal was to learn Spanish. And I did.

I also changed a lot during my time in Costa Rica. For the first time, I became close friends with people from the LGBTQ community and learned what it was like to have to hide your love for another human being.

I also met people from all over Latin America who made a living selling handcrafted jewelry and trinkets to tourists. I joined them for several months, traveling within Costa Rica and up through Central America, making just enough to pay for food, lodging and bus fare. I remember one day in Panajachel, Guatemala. We had just arrived into town after a two-day bus ride through Central America. We needed to sell some jewelry, so we could buy something to eat and pay for a place to sleep that night. We put our cloth down on the ground along a path where a lot of tourists passed and started to set out our product. Soon, a couple of women from the town came by and started yelling at us. I didn't understand what was going on. My friend explained to me that they were telling us to get out of their town. We didn't want trouble, so we moved down the street a ways, and we did sell a few trinkets that day.

I feel really stupid admitting this, but it wasn't until a few years later when I went to Guatemala to work with some women handcrafters that I truly understood why those women had been so upset we were selling our jewelry in their town. They were trying to feed their children. Selling products to tourists for them was their livelihood. For me, it was a way to see the world. But even though I didn't fully understand why the women were so angry with us at the time, I did recognize the power of those women, and I was so impressed by them. So, years later when I went back to work with them, I knew I wasn't walking in to "help." I was walking in to collaborate and reciprocate.

POWER

Power is defined as *"The capacity or ability to direct or influence the behavior of others or the course of events."*[18] Remember the question I ask the groups I speak to: "Have you ever looked out your car window (either literally and figuratively), seen a problem and thought, *someone, should do something about that?"* Power is doing something about it. Power is my friend Kathy O'Keefe standing up to a town council that continuously makes decisions that hurt a community by running and being elected to town council, even though she had never before considered running for office. Power are my clients, Teri, Shawna and Ashley (a mother/sisters trio), who, seeing that women in their community need more support in order to reach for higher life and career goals, started Jam Program, a community-building program where multi-generational women are encouraged to "be brave" and to go after higher goals within a supportive network of women.

Power is also about the control we have over our own lives and resources. Power is about being able to live the life that feels right for you. Power is leaving a job that does not appreciate you or does not help you grow.

My client, Teresa, is embracing her power to create monumental change in the world and in her life. Teresa recently took a huge step in setting her better-world idea in motion.

"For a year I tooled around with an idea to spark a movement of people capable of standing up to hate in America—but I hesitated to leave the security of a position that had grown too small for me. In order for me to make the leap to launch the transformative change I believed needed to happen in this world, I was going to have to change the way I saw myself. I was going to have to stretch out of my comfort zone and use my own voice. But my fears stopped me from quitting my job and striking out on my own. Kirsten helped me to tackle the really practical problems that posed as the kryptonite to my vision. She gave me concrete examples of how to earn money that helped me see how making the leap made sense. Working with Kirsten, I had the dedicated time and space to redirect my mojo and to use my voice to accomplish the change I wanted to see happen in the world. Today, I have left the job that was too small for me; set up a consulting business and I signed my first client to generate money; and I've put together the 3-year action plan to spark a movement of people to stand up to hate and am in the process of filing all the paperwork to make this vision an official organization."

I love that I could add so much value to Teresa's journey within only a few months. But really, what I did was help Teresa discover that she has the POWER to do EVERYTHING that she wants to do (and more).

Is power a motivator for you? Maybe you want to feel more in control of how your philanthropy is used? Maybe you recently retired from a high-powered job and are missing the power you once held? Maybe events happening in your community make you feel like you are powerless?

SOCIAL

One of my clients recently told me, "I want to spend my time with people who are passionate about making change in the world. My colleagues are nice, but they really don't seem to care about anything outside of doing their job and going home to watch *The Bachelor*. I feel such a disconnect, and it makes me sad."

Belonging to a movement, business or organization aligned with your vision for your community and your life is a way to build a social structure that fits with how you want to show up in the world.

I'm not saying that you should build a "social bubble" around you of people who only think, act and talk like you. One of the beautiful elements of changemaking work is that it gives you an opportunity to meet and get to know people who you might not otherwise interact with. As you build your tribe of co-collaborators, your community will expand in ways you could not imagine.

I think about this when I look at my Facebook feed. On one post, I'll have comments from my artist friend, Daniella in Bolivia, who I worked with on several projects; from my friend, Tor, a man in Afghanistan, who was my driver when I worked there; and from my friend, Renu in India, whom I met in a photography course in New York City. My social life is so much more diverse and rich than it would be if I had stayed in the small town in Upstate New York, where I grew up.

A social motivation can also include recognition. Perhaps you want your kids to be proud of you. Maybe it's important that you serve as a role model for your friends and family. I was recently leading a workshop for the Business Council for Peace (Bpeace) and when I asked the group what social motivations they had for being a "Skillanthropist" (what Bpeace calls their volunteers), one woman spoke up and said that Bpeace offers her experiences that allow her to connect with like-minded people who care deeply about the health of the world.

Go Deeper

1. What would you put on the Legacy Wall?

2. Imagine that you are being given a prestigious award. It can be a community award or a Nobel Prize; it's up to you. Your good friend is introducing you to the audience and outlining your great vision that you had for your community and how you accomplished it. What does she say?

3. What are your motivations for wanting to make change in your life and your community?

CHAPTER 5:

Discover Your Sweet Spot

*"Sweet Spot: an optimum point or combination
of factors or qualities."*
- Dictionary.com

Dayna Reggero knew she wanted to do something about climate change. She knew it wasn't only one type of person experiencing climate change. It's all of us who are impacted.

"It comes to your backyard. It comes to the children we want to be healthy and safe. It comes to the bird that you love to see every spring. It's comes to the food we eat and the farmers that want to be able to hand their farms down to their children."

Dayna saw that people wanted to talk about climate change and they wanted to listen to the impacts that were affecting change on a local level. So, she began to dig in deep and learn about the issue of climate change from all sides of the story. Dayna turned to what she knew best, film and media— (she had been a TV personality when she was younger) —and began to film people's stories.

Then she realized she was on to something. People wanted to have real, personal conversations about climate change beyond the standard arguments we hear on the news.

Dayna formalized her idea and founded the Climate Listening Project in 2014. Since then, Dayna and her team have traveled across the United States and around the world "to explore the connections that are important to each of us: family, faith, business, community; weaving together the latest science with inspiring stories from around the globe."

> *"I think that right now, people can do whatever they want. So, if you have an idea, do something. Get it together, know what it is. All people can do is say no. Just keep pitching."*

Today, Climate Listening Project stories can be found in 120 places online and have been screened at local events, film festivals, conferences and churches around the world. Her *Cultivating Resilience* videos were screened at the International Paris Climate Talks. Dayna's first feature documentary *The Wood Thrush Connection* was honored as the *Best Short Documentary Winner* at the *2017 Belize International Film Festival*. In 2018, she won the Storyteller Award for Best Documentary Short Film at the Micropolitan Film Festival.

When I interviewed Dayna for my Ordinary, Extraordinary Changemaker story series, I asked her what advice she has for someone who has an idea for creating change in their community.

"I think that right now, people can do whatever they want. So, if you have an idea, do something. Get it together, know what it is. All people can do is say no. Just keep pitching."

This chapter will help you learn how to find your sweet spot as a Changemaker no matter your project or passion. The problems we face as a society are complex, and you can't do everything. So, let's figure out what you can do, and how you can make the biggest impact yet still feel the greatest satisfaction as you fit into the solution. You will get clearer on how to take your idea and actually create change.

Become a Detective

If you are going to put in the time, effort and resources to become a Changemaker, don't you want to actually change lives?

A few years ago, I met a woman, Diane, in the lobby of a hotel in Guatemala City. She looked quite sad, so I asked her if there was something I could do to help. Diane looked at me, paused, and then told me that she was embarrassed and sad and she just wanted to go home to Florida. "What happened?" I asked. She told me that at her church she had heard about a young woman in a village in Guatemala who had a disability and couldn't walk. Wanting to do something to help, Diane raised $400 from her friends at church to buy a wheelchair for the young woman. She explained that the people who go to her church don't have a lot of money and it was a big deal for them to help someone they didn't even know. That day, during a mission trip to Guatemala, Diane brought the wheelchair to the young woman's home. The young woman smiled and thanked her but said she couldn't use the chair. There were no paved roads in her village, and the path to her house wasn't passable in a wheelchair. Diane hadn't taken the time to understand what the young woman needed before she'd acted. "Not only did I look really insensitive in front of this young woman who I really wanted to help," Diane told me, "but now I have to go back to my friends at church and tell them what happened."

Part of being an effective Changemaker is digging in deep and learning about the problem you are trying to fix or improve. This means learning about the problem from *all* sides of the issue.

This research can get uncomfortable. It can push you outside of your comfort zone. And that's when change happens. Your best ideas will come to you outside of your comfort zone. When you stretch your knowledge, experiences and points of view, you'll see more clearly how you can fit into the solution.

> *Part of being an effective Changemaker is digging in deep and learning about the problem you are trying to fix or improve. This means learning about the problem from all sides of the issue.*

It's comfortable to hang out with like-minded people. It feels good to have your beliefs validated. Sometimes this is exactly what you need. But if you are serious about learning about an issue and creating change, you will likely need to step outside of your comfort zone and seek out situations that force you to look at your issue from another angle.

You don't have to embrace discomfort by immersing yourself in a week-long conference with people whose viewpoints are 180 degrees apart from your own. You can begin (and end) by joining a group aligned with your beliefs but who offer a different perspective.

For example, if you are interested in promoting local organic farming, reach out to a restaurant association in your area to gain a better understanding of restaurateurs' challenges and interests in sourcing products.

Why is this important? Let's take LGBTQ rights as an example. I am a queer woman and, for the most part, am very open about who I am and who I love. I have, however, experienced discrimination and rejection for being who I am. Sometimes, this has been slightly annoying and easy to brush off. When these attitudes came from my family or close friends, it has been extremely painful. A few times, it has been downright scary, when I felt like I was in danger of physical harm on a Brooklyn street when a group of men harassed my girlfriend and me.

So, talking to people who believe that being queer is wrong and that I don't have the same rights to marry, adopt children or even simply to live my life is not something I want to do. I tend to stay clear of these conversations because, frankly, I think they are redundant and pointless.

Yet, I know that walking away from these conversations means missing a chance to understand the other person's viewpoint. Staying and having the conversation, regardless of how aggravating or painful it may be, might allow me to build empathy and compassion with the other person and vice versa.

But I also see another reason for having these conversations. I can be a secret agent gathering information to be used in the fight for what I believe is right.

To be clear, I would much prefer to gain this insight through dialogue that can be used to bring people around to understanding that justice and equity is not only the right thing to do, it also creates healthier communities. But, I'm not against leveraging what I learn to fight for the change I want to see in my community either.

> *I ask my clients when they are digging deeper into the problem they are trying to address is, "Whose voice are you not hearing in discussions around the issue?"*

If my vision is to make my community a place where all people are accepted and welcomed regardless of sexual orientation, identity, race, language, ability, immigration status or socioeconomic level, understanding the resistance to my vision will help me come up with unorthodox ways to overcome or bypass that resistance to get what I want.

One of the questions I ask my clients when they are digging deeper into the problem they are trying to address is, "Whose voice are you not hearing in discussions around the issue?" This includes what part of the story are you not seeing in the media?

Pavni Guharoy recognized that people of color have long been stereotyped by mainstream media. So, Pavni set out with her camera to create positive imagery of communities of color. She started ImpactLens Photography in 2016 to show the other side of the story that is usually portrayed in mainstream media, particularly in the African American, immigrant and LGBTQ communities.

"I think mainstream media, which is very dominated by white reporters and white photographers, has continued to frame people of color, visually and narratively, in an intentionally negative way.

I almost I feel like there's a hangover of colonization where the impression is, even before you understand what that person is doing, if you're black then you must be of a certain income class or if you're Latino you must be working a certain type of job.

I feel it's those visual stereotypes that get in the way of truly getting to know someone or respect someone and be kind.

I live in a black city, and I'm surrounded by amazing men who are just living their lives the best that they can, and they're doing really great at it. But mainstream media never focus on those stories. The media always picks up the men that are getting shot, the men that are, you know, breaking into neighborhoods or men that are abandoning their families, men that are lazy and sitting on street corners.

The black men's photo project I have started this year is specifically trying to defy stereotypes that I think white mainstream media has about black men.

I'm also photographing the LGBT[Q] community, transwomen, sex workers. I feel it's important to show those people as joyful and real people. They're not living in the shadows of society.

I feel like we visually created this social class system where if you look a certain way, you get treated a certain way.

If you're gay or you're dark-skinned, or you're not well-dressed, or you speak a certain way. I feel like there's a lot to be done in terms of defying visual stereotypes.

I feel like if we start to look at people differently, we will inevitably start to treat them differently."

Find the Gap

The other reason to dig deeply into the problem you want to solve or the change you want to create is because in gaining knowledge and understanding, you will see more clearly the gap where you can add value.

In Chapter 3, I talked about how Changemakers don't recreate the wheel. They look critically and openly at a problem and find solutions or improve on existing solutions.

What is already being done by other organizations, the government and the private sector? What is working well? Who is getting results? More importantly, where is there a gap in services? Where is a need not being filled? How can you fill that gap, instead of duplicating the work that is already being done?

Here's a quick example. Say you want to do something about hunger in your community, but you aren't sure what to do or where you should start. You could start a food pantry, but there are already a couple of food pantries run by local churches.

Then, you start learning more about why hunger is a problem in your community. You pay a visit to a pastor at a local church where a lot of newly-arrived immigrants attend services. You find out that many of his parishioners have a hard time finding jobs that pay enough to cover rent and food. Many of them don't have skills beyond doing manual labor or working entry-level jobs in fast food places.

You begin to think, *what if I created a business employing people and helping them develop skills, so they could secure better jobs or even start their own businesses?*

You decide if you leverage your startup business skills you could establish a community bakery that employs people, teaches them business and trade skills and provides food to people in need. And you would be adding value to solving a community problem instead of creating another food pantry that would compete for the same resources.

I've been a fan of Hot Bread Kitchen (HBK), based in Harlem, New York since I heard about it several years ago. Jessamyn Rodriguez founded it in 2007 to create economic opportunities through careers in food and she "...envisions a food system that equitably compensates talent and sustains a diverse workforce while celebrating culinary tradition and innovation."[19] They offer paid on-the-job training for women from around the world so that they can learn culinary skills, English as a second language, science and math. Then, they place all graduates of the program, who want jobs, in fair wage positions. HBK also has a culinary business incubator program, HBK Incubates, that helps food entrepreneurs launch businesses. HBK Incubates offers their participants commercial kitchen access, business development support, a culinary community and market access opportunities.[20]

Your Theory of Change

Often, when I first talk to my clients about their ideas for going beyond giving to charity to create change in their communities, they tell me all the activities they have in mind and their bigger vision for the impact they will create. They want to teach kids theater, hold workshops for white woman to learn about the experiences of women of color or start a foundation to "give back" to the community.

One well-meaning, enthusiastic man told me that he started an organization that takes kids who have suffered trauma to Disney World so that they will live healthy, happy lives. The problem is that there is a huge gap between the activity (taking kids to Disney World) and the impact (healthy, happy lives). There is a lot more required to ensure that kids lead healthy happy lives, especially children who have experienced some form of trauma.

I don't say this to criticize a heart-centered action but because I see the lack of attention paid to how lives could be changed as a missed opportunity and the difference between creating a little bit of impact and transformative change in the lives of children.

This is where your Theory of Change comes in. Theory of Change (ToC) is a methodology that is used in nonprofits, governments and philanthropy to create a roadmap for how organizations create social change. It can get a bit wonky, so I've kept it somewhat simple for the purpose of this book. If you are interested in learning more about Theory of Change, www.theoryofchange.org is a good resource.

For now, think of your Theory of Change as "the big how" you are going to create social, economic or environmental change—how you are going to change lives. It starts with the ultimate goal you are trying to reach and then examines what conditions have to be in place to make that goal a reality. In other words, what has to happen in a child's life to help her heal from trauma and live a healthy, happy life? Your answer might include a trip to Disney World, but before you decide on that activity, you'll want to understand how it will help you reach your end goal.

Let's look at the example of one of my first clients to help us understand better how this works. (I've simplified this case study for the purposes of this book). My client, Maria, wanted to start a community center where people would take classes and workshops, join business development groups and come together in fellowship and community. Her vision was that kids and adults would live healthier and happier lives and members of the community would support each other in activities like expanding their businesses, running for office, building a stronger Parent-Teachers Association and providing support for people struggling in the community.

The problem, and one of the reasons Maria decided to work with me was that she had the challenge of defining and communicating exactly how the community center adds "investment-worthy value" to its members and to potential investors. Investment-worthy value means that the center is providing such a high level of value to its members that members will invest their money and time to join the center. In other words, the results of the program have to be quantifiable and meaningful to Maria's "clients," the members of the community center. This doesn't necessarily mean that all members see a financial return on investment (ROI) because that may not be important to each member. Some members want their ROI to be a healthier, less stressed lifestyle or they want to find peace of mind in coming together with their neighbors to create safe streets.

To understand how to provide "investment-worthy value" for her members, Maria needed to start by getting clear on two key questions:

1. Who are her ideal clients and what are their problems?

2. Which problems will the community center try to solve?

(Whether you are starting a for-profit or non-profit changemaking initiative or if you haven't defined that yet, these two questions are just as important to answer.)

The answer to the second question is the starting point of my client's Theory of Change.

Maria identified two overarching problems she wanted to help her members solve:

1. They wanted to reach new levels of success in their careers, businesses and academic achievements.

2. They wanted to live in a more economically viable, safe and inclusive community so they and their families could thrive.

So, Maria's ultimate goal, the impact she wanted to create in her community through the community center, was a viable, safe and inclusive community where community members achieved personal and professional goals.

The question then becomes, how does she achieve that goal? *What conditions have to be in place to create that impact?* From talking to people in her community, potential community center members, and by looking at how other towns had created similar results, she knew that some of the conditions that needed to be in place to create the impact included elements like; a supportive business environment, quality education in the local schools, career guidance and opportunities and a police force that worked in partnership with community members.

By the way, you can also use the Theory of Change to make a map of the problem or issue you research to identify where there are gaps and where you can step in to be part of the solution. You can even use it to examine your own life and figure out where you want to go.

Once you have identified the conditions that need to be in place to reach your ultimate goal, you'll be able to design the activities and interventions that will lead to the outcomes that will help get you to your goal. This is the fun part, and you'll have a chance to do this in Chapter 7. I'm going to show you how you expand your Theory of Change, so it becomes a tool that guides your actions. Think of it as a blueprint for how you are going to bring about the change you want to see in your community.

Go Deeper

1. What is already being done by other organizations, the government and the private sector to fix the issue you have identified? What is working well? Who is getting results?

2. Where is there a gap in services? Where is there a need that is not being filled? How can you fill that gap, instead of duplicating the work they are already doing?

3. Building on the gap you have identified, what are three ideas for the ultimate impact you can create in your community?

4. What investment-worthy value can you provide for the beneficiaries of and investors in your ideas?

PART 3:

From Idea to Impact

CHAPTER 6:

The Lives You'll Change

*"Cocreate: To create (something) by working
with one or more others."*
- Merriam Webster

Let's get real for a minute. You can't help every person, animal and tree on this planet. It's simply impossible. That's an obvious statement. It is also what I often have to remind my clients.

It is normal to look at all the problems in our communities and the people and animals in the natural world that are suffering and want to do something about it. That's part of what makes you a caring human being.

In Chapter 3, you narrowed in on the one or two issues that are the most important to you. In the last chapter, you thought about how you are going to bring about change. In this chapter, you'll narrow in on who you want to reach through your work.

This chapter is about getting clear on who you want to help, both directly and indirectly through your changemaking work. It is also about understanding all the stakeholders who will be involved in creating the impact you want to make.

Think of it as the "people chapter." We are going to delve into what people you are going to help and what people you need to help you help people. Of course, you can also think of it as the people and dog/cat/bird/elephant/trees chapter if your vision is to help animals or the natural world.

Whether you want to focus on changing the lives of children, making our communities more equitable or creating a city full of beautiful, life-giving murals, a solid general rule is to start out with a smaller target area (whether that's measured in lives or miles), and then to test your theory of change before you expand to reach more people.

Map Your Stakeholders

In 2006, I had the opportunity to architect a concept for a women's design center in Kabul, Afghanistan. The idea was to implement a business incubator program for women who were skilled in creating clothing and handcrafts to give them culturally appropriate opportunities in which to build businesses around that would help support their families. The incubator would assist the women in designing and selling products in the local expatriate market in Kabul and outside the country in markets like Dubai, Europe and the United States. On paper, it sounded promising, and we were given the funding to set up the design center.

I didn't have a lot of experience working in Afghanistan. And I had only been there for a couple of weeks doing an assessment of the handcraft sector before I wrote the concept for the design center. Afghanistan is a very complicated place, and I definitely did not have a good understanding of the stakeholders that would be needed to get the design center up and running, let alone who would make it a success.

To be clear, the basic idea of designing products and finding markets for them is fairly standard all over the world. I also had a team of U.S. and European experts working with me on the project.

Unfortunately, not understanding three key stakeholders when I launched the program led to the closing of the project a year after it started.

The first stakeholders were the women leaders who ran the women's federation where the design center was housed. I assumed, based on information I had been given, that they were 100% behind the design center from the beginning. That was a gross assumption on my part. They harbored resentment that the plan for the center had been basically dropped in their lap. They had their own ideas for a business incubator program and wanted to have a say in it. And they also had other priorities and ideas for how the limited funding allocated for women's development should be spent. By the time I realized this, the damage had been done, and a collaborative relationship was never truly established. Without their buy-in, it was hard to get anything done. Strike one.

The second group of stakeholders that I overlooked were local design consultants. Because I worked for an organization that typically targeted U.S. and European markets, I was used to interacting with designers from those markets. What I didn't realize was that many of the local designers in Kabul had been educated and had lived in the U.S. and Europe. They were very capable of designing products to fit those markets. I made the mistake of hiring international consults instead of leveraging the talent that was in the country. As you can imagine, this did not go over well with the local consultants. I don't blame them. It was insulting. One woman even sent an email to the design community in Kabul shaming our practices. Ouch. Strike two.

Then there were the donors, the third set of stakeholders. The project was funded by the United States Agency for International Development (USAID), but the money went through an organization for which we were a subcontractor. To make a long story short, the other organization decided to pull its program out of Afghanistan. I assumed the funding for the design center would then flow directly to our organization and we would keep the design center alive. I was wrong. The funding was redirected to another organization which had its own ideas for women's economic development, and they pulled the funding for the design center. Strike three.

In all three situations, I hadn't taken the time to fully understand the stakeholders who could have a greater impact on the design center.

———————

Completing a stakeholder analysis so that you understand who the various players are in and around your issue will help you find clarity on who you want to help and who you need to help you help more people.

Stakeholders are people, organizations, businesses, community leaders or government officials that could be impacted by your program or that have influence over your program. A stakeholder has a concern or interest in the problem you are trying to change. Depending on the scope of your issue, there can be a few stakeholders to thousands of stakeholders.

Completing a stakeholder analysis so that you understand who the various players are in and around your issue will help you find clarity on who you want to help and who you need to help you help more people. It sounds very daunting, but it doesn't have to be.

A stakeholder analysis will help you decide who you want to focus on in your work. This might seem obvious, but communities are complex and not taking the time to understand the stakeholders can delay or derail your project.

When I am working with a client on a new project, I guide them into making a map of all the stakeholders. It doesn't have to be a fancy map with lots of bells and whistles. A simple representation of the stakeholders, with a few empty slots for those you discover as you put action behind your idea, will suffice.

As an example, let's take a look at my client, Susanne. After a successful career as a neuroscientist, she began to mentor high school girls in science in the Bronx, where she lives. One of her mentees told her that she wasn't going to apply to a college science program because she didn't have any extracurricular activities to put on her application. After doing research into the type of programs available to students like her mentee, she found a gap in the STEM (Science, Technology, Engineering and Math) education programs in the local schools and decided it was an area where she could add value. Susanne founded EDSnaps (short for Education Snapshots). Susanne's goal is to increase diversity in the STEM workforce. As a woman with a long career in science, she felt strongly about this issue. She's doing this by providing personal and professional development for female-identifying high school students so that they have a better chance of entering university STEM programs. She's narrowed down her target audience to 9th and 10th-grade girls who attend public high schools in the Bronx.

In order to reach the students and further her goal, do you think there are other people, besides the students, she might need to reach? Yes! Parents, teachers, guidance counselors, school administrators, science and technology companies in the city and college admission professionals, to name a few.

This is what Susanne's stakeholder list looks like:

- Students - Have to attend and actively engage in the program.
- Teachers - Encourage students to attend EDSnaps. Incorporate EDSnaps prep and follow-up work into classroom curriculum.
- School Administrators - Inform teachers and guidance counselors of EDSnaps opportunity. Make physical space and resources available for EDSnaps program.
- Parents - Encourage children to attend program and to pursue college STEM careers. Allow children to attend program instead of getting summer/after school jobs or performing other household duties.

- Science and Tech Companies - Provide company tours, speakers and mentors for program.
- College Admission Staff – Recognize the value of students who go through EDSnaps program on college entrance applications.

Once you have identified the groups of people you could impact, you'll want to dig deeper to understand who they are.

1. What are the characteristics of these people?
2. Where are they, and where do they spend their time?
3. What is your relationship to them?
4. Where do they get their information?
5. What is important to them?
6. What are their interests?

Choose Your Beneficiaries

Once you've mapped out your stakeholders, you will want to decide who you will target as your clients or beneficiaries. These are an important subset of your stakeholders.

It can be argued that all of the stakeholders on Susanne's list play an important role in helping Susanne achieve her dream of creating a program that will eventually contribute to a more diverse STEM workforce. To that end, EDSnaps could choose to create programs for only the students, all of the stakeholders or some of the stakeholders.

Susanne could move the needle closer to achieving her goal if she provides workshops for the students, teachers, parents and tech companies. But that would be a lot of work, especially for a young organization with limited resources. It's also possible other organizations and companies are focused on working with parents, schools or technology companies to further the same goal and EDSnaps complements those programs. This is why, as we talked about in Chapter 5 identifying gaps in the marketplace and where you can add value is so important.

In Susanne's case, she began with a definition of her target client as high school and college-aged girls. But, after implementing her program, she realized most of the students who were showing up to her information sessions were 9th and 10th graders. For the most part, these students weren't old enough to hold part-time jobs and so more than likely they had the time to dedicate to the EDsnaps program.

Build Your Team

Changemaking is about community. It is about leveraging and combining skills, resources, networks, ideas and passion to solve problems that hurt our communities or to improve on existing solutions to the problems.

It is not up to you and only you to save the world. Unless you are literally a superhero (and even then, it's questionable), you can't do it by yourself. But you can combine your superpower with the superpowers of others and make an unstoppable team.

Changemaking is about community. It is about leveraging and combining skills, resources, networks, ideas and passion to solve problems that hurt our communities or to improve on existing solutions to the problems.

One of the biggest problems my clients face, especially when launching a new idea, is their internal critic. Most of us have that voice inside our head that tries to talk us out of ideas. The problem is that we listen to that voice, even when we've got a really great idea, and then we delay or miss our chance to change lives.

Well-meaning people in our lives also try to talk us out of taking risks. "Why would you leave that good job when you get paid really well?" "Why switch gears now when you've spent so much time and effort building your career?" "The problems in the world will always be there. There is nothing you can do to change that."

This is why it is so important to build a team around you that is going to cheer you on, give you honest and valuable feedback and help you keep going when you hit roadblocks. You want to include people who see your vision and want to play a part in helping you achieve it.

One way of building your team is finding collaborators and cocreators in the form of co-founders, board members, advisors and/or funders/investors.

It's also key to include a community outside of your team. One of the reasons I designed the Women's Changemaker Mentorship™ as a group program is because I knew the magic that happens when people come together to share their ideas would propel my clients' ideas forward at a much faster pace than if my clients worked alone. I've experienced this myself. When I first started my business, I invested in a business mentorship program that connected me with successful, generous businesswomen who understood my challenges and were there when I needed help getting over the mindset and business building hurdles that I encountered (and still do). I can't imagine doing the work I do without support from a powerful group of women.

One of the concerns that my clients share with me when they are starting to put their changemaking idea out into the world by talking to people is that they, "Don't want to bother people" by talking about their idea. I tell my clients to "speak to experts and people who might benefit from your changemaking idea." They reply: "I'm sure they don't want to help me. What if they think my idea is silly?"

Here's the truth. People love to be cocreators. If you look at all the people you meet and talk to as cocreators instead of as people who are doing you a favor, before you know it, you'll have a community of people who are excited about and invested in what you are trying to do.

Of course, you will find some people who don't want to talk or listen. Don't take it personally. It's not that your idea has no merit, or they think you are incapable. It's just that, for whatever reason, they don't want to be one of your cocreators—maybe lack of time, they aren't interested in the subject or what you are doing feeds into their own insecurities.

When I started writing this book, I reached out to about 60-70 people to interview. I simply said, "I'm writing a book about giving back. I would love to interview you about your experiences." Many people—about 50—immediately responded and were thrilled to be interviewed. For the most part, the interviews were filled with inspiration, information and encouragement. I loved talking to people. The conversations made me even more determined to write this book.

There were a few, however, who declined to speak with me. Early on I was excited because I had identified the person who I wanted to ask to write the foreword. I have admired her work for years and was encouraged when she initially responded to me for a request for an interview. But then I received a polite response from her assistant that she was unable to talk. I was disappointed until I realized her decision was not personal. She's busy and is on her own path to creating change. I figure she'll probably read this book at some point and realize she missed a unique opportunity.

People whose lives are directly impacted by the problem you are trying to address, may have had the experience of people coming to them with ideas, and these people may have taken up their time asking questions, then they may have gone on with their lives and not taken action on their ideas. Or worse, people may have started projects and abandoned them leaving the people in their community high and dry. Funding might have dried up, or well-meaning people may have discovered they aren't getting what they had anticipated out of the experience.

This is why, in my Women's Changemaker Mentorship™, I ask people to look deeply at their motivations for wanting to give back. I ask my clients to spend time thinking selfishly so they will have clarity about what they need to get to feel fulfilled in their changemaking work. I do this because if you are clear on your motivations and you design your changemaking initiative with those motivations in mind, you are more likely to stick with the work long-term.

You'll need a team to help you move your idea forward. Not everyone will be on your daily or even weekly call list. You won't even meet or talk to some stakeholders. Instead, you'll pull from the experiences they've written about in books, documentary films, articles and other resources to inform your work. You'll pay some cocreators for their services; some will become part of your board of directors or advisory board, some will be informal relationships whose "brains you pick" when you need a little help, and some you'll find in groups of like-minded people. Having this community is invaluable. Ideas grow and expand when fed by community. Collaborations happen, and more lives are changed when you work with other people, not to mention the friendships that are formed.

I have found that there are some common types of cocreators. Here is a definition of some of the cocreators and the roles they play in social impact work:

1. The Cheerleader - A person who believes in what you are trying to do and who supports you with their enthusiasm and attentive ear. She often will tell other people about what you are trying to do.

2. The Fundraiser - A person who has expertise in raising money, whether philanthropy, venture capital or other types of startup funds. This person isn't necessarily going to open doors to funding for you, but she can guide you on how the system works.

3. The Connector - A person who is well connected and can introduce you to people who can be a resource for you. One of the ways I add value to my clients is connecting and introducing them to people who can guide them and give them key information.

4. The Subject Matter Expert - A person who is a subject matter or location expert who can help you think through your strategies around a specific topic (e.g., STEM education in high school) or working in a specific location (e.g., Bronx high schools).

5. The Marketing Genius - A person who understands effective ways to get the word out about the work you are doing, through organic and paid means. In my business, receiving guidance on basic social media strategies has been really helpful.

6. The Mentor - A person who has built a social impact organization or business and can help guide you on the options available to develop your ideas.

7. Stakeholders - People who have a vested interest in the work you are trying to do. The more, the better.

8. The Donor/Investor - Before you even start asking for money, confirm the donor/investors who will be in your corner as cocreators and advisors. Doing so will make it a lot easier when you start raising money.

Go Deeper

1. Who are the key stakeholders you need to consider when designing your roadmap to create change?

2. Who are the beneficiaries of your changemaking work?

3. Who do you need and want on your changemaking team? What roles will they play?

4. What are the benefits of having a group to support you? How will you ask them to help you?

CHAPTER 7:

A Living, Breathing Plan

*"Roadmap: A detailed plan to guide
progress toward a goal."*
- Merriam Webster

One of my first clients, Latrice (not her real name), hired me to do a strategy session with her a year after she started an advocacy group to demand prison reform in her state. Latrice was great at laying out the big picture of the change they were going to make as a powerful group of concerned citizens. She had a gift for convincing people to join her efforts and, in some cases, to support them financially. She was a visionary! Within a few months, Latrice had a hundred people showing up to planning meetings. The problem was that, although Latrice was a compelling leader and visionary, she wasn't able to move her idea forward to action. The planning meetings were more like discussion meetings, where the same topics would be debated over and over again. But in between meetings, no action would be taken. During my strategy session with Latrice, I asked her about her biggest challenges. She told me that although she had started out strong and a lot of people supported what she was trying to do, a lot of people were starting to drop off. When I asked her why she thought that was, she said that people told her that they were frustrated with the lack of action. They didn't want to sit around and discuss the same issues over and over again. They wanted to do something! Latrice admitted with frustration and pain in her voice that she felt like she was failing and that she didn't have a plan for moving her ideas forward. She shared with me that she had no idea how to go from her vision to getting people to help her take action on that vision. I helped her get clarity around what she needed to move her idea forward, including asking for help and finding people who had skills that she didn't.

You've made the decision to change your life and community. You've gotten real with yourself about your motivations. You've figured out what skills you want to use, the impact you want to have and the lives you want to change. You've even started to gather your cocreators.

Now it's time to design the plan that is going to turn your dreams into action, so you can create the impact you want.

In this chapter, you are going to design a clearly defined and organized roadmap to get you where you want to go.

> *You begin by dreaming BIG about the change you want to see and then dreaming SMALL about one action you can take to make it happen.*

One of the challenges of starting a changemaking project is that it can feel so overwhelming that you do nothing. You don't know where to begin, and so you don't begin.

I'm going to tell you a little secret. None of us know where to begin. You begin by beginning. You begin by learning one small thing about an issue you care about. You begin by having one small conversation with someone who knows one little tidbit more than you do about the issue you care about. You begin by dreaming BIG about the change you want to see and then dreaming SMALL about one action you can take to make it happen.

Remember my client, Stephanie, who is working with moms who want to go back into the workforce? Stephanie listened into one of my free webinars and reached out to me almost immediately. She told me that after hearing what I had to say on my webinar, she knew I was the person who could help her figure out what to do with the idea she had been playing around with in her head for months. She recognized that I cared deeply about creating change in our communities and would be able to help her create change in her community. She had been trying to solidify what she wanted to do but quickly became overwhelmed by all of the information she needed to know. It was hard for Stephanie to know what the right decisions were to make.

"For a long time, I thought, who am I to start a business? I have learned that my skills hold considerable value and the experiences I've had since relaunching my career after raising four kids positions me on equal footing as other senior leaders in the room. What Kirsten really helped me with was being able to identify specifically what it is that I want to do. For so long, I was in a sort of free fall. I really wanted to help moms going back into the workforce finding meaningful careers in the non-profit sector but could not find the right vehicle to make that happen. I really understand now what's the best vehicle for me to create and accomplish my goals."

One of the requirements you need to address before you start working with me is to choose a shorter-term goal that you will design a project around. Why do I have clients focus on this shorter-term initiative instead of on the longer-term impact they want to make? Because I know that creating change requires putting one block on top of the other. It's just like building a skyscraper. Piece by piece, floor by floor.

But you also need an architectural blueprint that you can refer to as you build each floor, or in the case of your changemaking initiative, that will guide you as you reach each milestone. Your theory of change that you created in Chapter 5 informs your blueprint. Keep in mind it might change, and that is okay. As you move forward in your project and learn from what you are doing and from talking to others, it's normal for your ideas and plans to shift.

One of the key takeaways I learned was that you always design from the market backward. In other words, you look at what the market trends are, what consumers like, and then you design the products to fit the market.

With the idea that your plans will probably shift, you are going to create a plan or blueprint. Yes, this is the anchor document, but it is flexible.

When I start working with my clients who already have organizations or businesses, they first tell me about all the activities they have designed. When I ask how those activities lead to the greater impact they want to have in the world, they usually have a vague sense of how they are connected.

I get it. Designing and implementing activities is the fun part! But, if you are serious about creating change, the activities have to be intentionally designed to get you to your goal.

I went to the Fashion Institute of Technology in New York City for my undergraduate studies. My major was in marketing and international trade. One of the key takeaways I learned was that you always design from the market backward. In other words, you look at what the market trends are, what consumers like, and then you design the products to fit the market.

I saw this strategy in action when I worked with handcraft producers in El Salvador, Egypt and Afghanistan among other countries. Often, we were helping the artisans move their products into new international markets. So, we would hire designers from those markets, like the U.S., to help artisans design and produce products that the U.S. consumer would buy. I frequently thought how strange it must be for artisans in places like El Salvador to be asked to create products for the multi-billion-dollar pet market in the United States. Just imagine weaving Christmas-themed dog sweaters while sitting on the floor of a simple, dirt floor workshop outside San Salvador, where you spend your time merely trying to make money to buy school uniforms for your kids—never mind even thinking about buying clothes for the dog!

Design Your Roadmap

When I facilitate the design of multi-million-dollar, multi-country international development programs, with 15-25 people in the room speaking 2-3 different languages, I use a process to condense all the ideas and goals into an actionable plan.

The tool I most often use is based on the Theory of Change, just as you learned about in Chapter 5. I have simplified the process a bit since I typically work with people who are starting new projects or working to grow their initiative, not people who are building out multi-million-dollar programs.

This is an incredibly useful tool, whatever stage you are in with your business, organization or passion project. It will lead you through the thinking of what you are trying to achieve, what you have to do to get there, who and what resources you need, and how you'll measure your progress along the way.

Think of it as creating your own roadmap for your changemaking project, whether it's just an idea in your head or a business you have already created, whether you are interested in becoming a social intrapreneur, finding a job that will better fit your changemaking goals or launching a new program to help people in your community—this tool will help you get your ducks in order.

Here's a template for your roadmap. I'm going to explain all the elements in a moment.

Inputs	Stakeholders	Activities	Outputs	Outcomes	Impact

Just like what I learned about in marketing in college and what I referenced a few pages back—to design for the market backward--when designing your project, start at the end (the impact you want to have) and design backward.

YOUR IMPACT

Your impact is what you want to make happen, the change you want to see, that is the result of solving a problem. This is what you identified in Chapter 5. Impact is the result of your hard work, the lives changed, the people helped, and the communities transformed. Impacts are usually longer-term and broader in scope.

Remember my client, Maria who wanted to start a community center? The impact that she wanted to create was a viable, safe and inclusive community where community members achieve personal and professional goals.

YOUR OUTCOMES

To create impact, you first need to facilitate the conditions that will lead to the impact. These conditions are your Outcomes. Outcomes are the short-term or intermediate changes that result from your program, products and services. In addition to being more shorter term than impact, outcomes also can generally be measured at the individual or group level, whereas impact typically has a broader reach (community, society, environment). In your Theory of Change, the Outcomes have to be in place for the wider impact to result.

For example, Maria identified the following outcomes for her community center:

- A supportive business environment
- Quality education in the local schools
- Career guidance and opportunities
- Police force working in partnership with community members.

YOUR OUTPUTS

Now, in your theory of change, what has to happen for your program or service to result in your intended outcomes and impact? Outputs are what you produce or deliver. The definition of outputs may include the number of kids you mentor, the number of households who start using your clean energy product or the number of women who go through your program who are elected to office.

I like to think of this section as the "number of widgets" portion of your roadmap. When I designed large conservation projects, we would include factors like the number of farmers trained, the number of cacao plants planted, and the number of new conservation methods adopted.

Some of the outputs for Maria and her community center were:

- Number of community members attending business development classes
- Number of business owners actively participating in the Chamber of Commerce
- Number of parents completing education activism trainings
- Number of new jobs created in and around the community

YOUR ACTIVITIES

Now for the fun part. You can identify the activities you are going to do that will lead to the outputs, outcomes and ultimate impact you want to create.

Activities can generally be divided into five categories. Depending on your vision, skills and motivation, you might add some additional categories.

- Creating
- Teaching

- Connecting
- Influencing
- Catalyzing

Some of Maria's community center activities included:

- Creation of a teen lounge
- Entrepreneurship classes
- Community Affinity Group Meetups
- Political Candidate Forums

YOUR STAKEHOLDERS

In Chapter 6, you mapped your stakeholders and identified your beneficiaries. You can plug in who you are going to target with your activities here.

Maria's stakeholders included:

- Town, county, state and national government officials
- Local businesses

Her beneficiaries were the members of the community.

YOUR INPUTS

Inputs are the resources you will need to have or to acquire to implement your activities. Resources mean money, materials, workers and so on. This is where you will build your budget, decide who you need to hire and purchase the materials and supplies you will need to carry out your activities. This is where my clients often start to take a serious look at how much they have to invest to make their dream come alive.

Get Comfortable with the Money

But, Kirsten! Where do I get the money to make all this happen?

Spoiler Alert! I'm not going to go into the nitty-gritty of fundraising, whether you want to raise philanthropic (i.e., donations) or investment capital. Tons of quality resources are available on the internet to help you think through how to find money for changemaking.

But before we get any further into this topic, I do want to spend some time talking about the sheer beauty of raising money to create change. Yes, I said *beauty*.

Several years ago, I met two women for breakfast at an upscale but quaint hotel on the Upper East Side of Manhattan. They were the heads of a small foundation, and I was there to ask them to help fund a poverty alleviation program in Central America. I hadn't slept well the night before, but had tossed and turned, thinking about how I was going to "pop the question." I don't know why this prospect made me so nervous. I had asked for money plenty of times before. In retrospect, I think it was because for most of my career as a fundraiser, up until that point, I had asked institutions for money (foundations, government agencies, corporations). So, this felt different. More personal. Technically the women represented a foundation, but it was *their* money I was requesting, not the government's or stockholders'.

I realized as I lie there trying to sleep, that I was nervous because I was *embarrassed* to ask for money. I felt like I was about to ask a colleague if I could borrow $50,000 to buy myself a fancy new car.

> *You are not asking for money for you. You are asking for the people you are trying to help and the communities you are trying to change.*

140

Fundraisers get a bad rap. In many cases, it's a thankless job. Your colleagues love you when times are good, and funding is flowing, and they blame you when times are bad, and funding is scarce. Donors avoid you. I always used to joke that if I was talking to an annoying person at a cocktail party, all I had to do was mention that I was a fundraiser and he would quickly make his exit from our conversation.

But raising money can be incredibly rewarding and exciting. And there is one thing you have to remember for it to be beautiful.

You are not asking for money for you. You are asking for the people you are trying to help and the communities you are trying to change. Whether you are asking for an investment as the CEO of an organic cosmetics company that is changing the way teenagers accept themselves or you are an artist crowdfunding an arts program for people with post-traumatic stress disorder, *you are asking for money to change lives.*

This might seem like simple advice, but I can't tell you how many people confide in me: "I can't raise money. I would be so ashamed to ask anyone for money."

Get it over it. This isn't about you.

I asked for the $50,000 at that breakfast meeting. The women said, "Yes," and I said, or rather blurted in one long sentence, "Oh my gosh, thank you so much I was so afraid to ask you I didn't sleep half the night worrying about our meeting this money means so much to our organization we are going to be able to help more women feed and send their kids to school thank you thank you thank you." One of the women studied me like she was trying to figure out whether someone had spiked my coffee, while the other woman just laughed. I guess I had broken some rule of fundraiser decorum with my babbling.

The worst that can happen when you ask someone for money to support your changemaking work is they will say no. If they do, remember it's not personal.

A couple of weeks later, I saw one of the women at a conference, and we sat down for a cup of tea. She told me how she had grown up with a lot of money in a community where a lot of people lived a working-class life and had very little money to spare. She always felt different from the other kids at school. When she was in high school and weighing which colleges to apply to, she was surprised to find out that a lot of her classmates weren't even considering college because their families couldn't afford it. Classmates who were as smart as she was, if not smarter, were going to work in the mills and fisheries in the area instead of following their dreams to become lawyers and business leaders. This guilt over having money was so intense; it lasted well into her adult life.

Giving money to help people, she told me, was her way of overcoming the guilt she'd grown up feeling. She told me that although sometimes it became overwhelming and could get a bit irritating, she was grateful when people asked her for money to support proven initiatives that change people's (and animals') lives.

So, like I said, get over it. It's not about you. The worst that can happen when you ask someone for money to support your changemaking work is they will say no. If they do, remember it's not personal.

That said, there are proven methods of fundraising, whether it's for a non-profit or for-profit initiative, that you will need to learn if you are going to fund your dream. I focus more on helping some of my clients learn how to cultivate the right type of donor, while I teach other clients how to offer their services and programs to their ideal clients at the right price.

Choose a Structure (or Don't)

Most people start their give-back journey with what house they are going to build. I want you to start with the lives you are going to change.

Once you figure out the who, what and how of creating change in your community, you will have a better idea of the type of legal structure you will want to use to house your changemaking initiative.

I'm going to let you in on a secret. Not all Changemakers start non-profits, and not all non-profits make change. A non-profit is, at the end of the day, simply a legal structure.

A lot of people call me because they have already paid an attorney to set up a non-profit and now they have NO IDEA what to do with it, or worse, they find out it's not the right structure to house what they want to do.

Most people start their give-back journey with what house they are going to build. I want you to start with the lives you are going to change.

I know what you're thinking. *Wait, what? I thought we were talking about helping people and changing the world. Aren't non-profits the way to do that?* Not necessarily. As I talked about in the Introduction, there are many options these days that can be leveraged to make a difference. Non-profits are no longer the only option. There is no rule stating that to create impact in your community you must use a charitable initiative. You can choose from many ways to give back, especially in the beginning when you don't quite know what you are doing. Also, setting up and maintaining a non-profit costs money. So, do your research before committing the time and expense to "build your house."

When Teri Dankovich and her business partner started Folia Water to bring their paper-based water filter to the world, they spent the first couple of years—including time and money—starting the non-profit. Then, an attorney helped them understand that a for-profit, B corporation would be a better option. Choosing the wrong option can cost you valuable time and money, and it can affect the impact made. But as I mentioned in the Introduction, over the past decade, several alternative structures for social change initiatives have become available, and they are changing the way the world thinks about charity and community development.

Here is a list of some of these options:

- Non-profit
- Foundation
- Social enterprise
- Fiscal sponsor
- LLC and LLP
- B Corporation
- A new program within an existing organization

NON-PROFIT

You might have heard of the term 501(c)(3) used to describe your local charity. This is only one type of what is considered a tax-exempt organization according to the Internal Revenue Service. But, there are 29 types of tax-exempt organizations. The type that is right for you depends on different factors like your mission, what type of activities you will carry out and whether you will be involved in political activities. It's a bit complicated so you will definitely want to talk to an attorney to help you figure out the best type for you.

FOUNDATION

A foundation is a nonprofit corporation or charitable trust that gives money, in the form of grants, to other non-profits, individuals and institutions for "scientific, educational, cultural, religious, or other charitable purposes."[21] There are two types of foundations: private foundations and grantmaking public charities.

Remember my client, the finance professional who wanted to start a foundation? A foundation was a good fit for him because he simply wanted to give money to organizations doing changemaking work in his community.

SOCIAL ENTERPRISE

Social enterprises use business principles to bring about financial, social and environmental impact in markets and communities where traditional markets and government are not meeting the needs of all people. Social enterprises can be for-profit, non-profit or a hybrid. VisionSpring, whose efforts bring affordable eyeglasses to millions of people, is an example of a social enterprise.

FISCAL SPONSOR

A fiscal sponsor is a tax-exempt organization offering their legal and tax-exempt status to an organization that does not have tax-exempt status so that the sponsored organization can receive funding and donations and extend tax exemptions to its donors. Fiscal sponsorship is a great option for newly formed organizations that haven't yet received their tax-exempt status or do not meet the requirement of many institutional donors to be in business for 2-3 years before they will fund an organization.

LIMITED LIABILITY COMPANY OR LIMITED LIABILITY PARTNERSHIP

Many of my clients start for-profit initiatives that have the goal of also doing good in their community. They often choose to register as a Limited Liability Company (LLC) or a Limited Liability Partnership, especially if they plan to have a revenue stream that does not include soliciting charitable donations.

B CORPORATION

B Corporations (Benefit Corporations or B Corps) are certified businesses that meet the highest standards of verified social and environmental performance, public transparency, and legal accountability to balance profit and purpose. Twenty-nine U.S. States recognize B Corporations as a legal form of a corporation. Patagonia and Warby Parker are certified B Corps. There are 2,000 B Corps in 140 industries in 50 countries.[22]

PROJECT WITHIN AN EXISTING ORGANIZATION

Without a doubt, there are likely to be many existing nonprofit organizations in your area. If you have successfully identified a gap in the marketplace and designed a program to fill that gap, you may want to discuss a partnership with an existing organization. It may even make sense to partner with a for-profit company. In many cases, this will allow you to start changing lives more quickly by focusing on implementing activities, instead of dealing with the expense and logistics of starting a new organization.

Go Deeper

1. What impact do you want to have?
2. What outcomes have to happen to create the impact?

3. What outputs do you need to create the outcomes?

4. What activities will create the desired outputs?

5. What inputs will you need to do your activities?

<u>Workbook Bonus: Theory of Change Worksheet</u>

6. What beliefs about money that you currently have will you need to change to create the impact you want to create?

7. What type(s) of structures seem like a good fit for you? Why?

CHAPTER 8:

Make It Happen

"Believe: To have a firm conviction as to the goodness, efficacy, or ability of something."
-Merriam Webster

Natalie Egan is obsessed with solving the problem of inequality. Natalie experienced bias, discrimination and hatred for the first time when, after 40 years of living life as a cisgender white man with all the privilege it brings, she came out as a transgender woman.

"When I transitioned, I experienced visceral hatred for just being me for the first time. I had this really nasty altercation with another customer at Starbucks. It was like a dagger in my chest that they just twisted before they laughed. I remember thinking to myself, *Wow. If that person only knew what I've been through and what I've done to people trying to conform.*"

Natalie could have accepted her new reality, that people were going to judge her and hate her just for being herself. She could have said, "There's nothing I can do about this, so let me live my life." But after that experience in Starbucks, Natalie thought, *if that person could just walk in my shoes for one day, if they could just understand my lived experience, they wouldn't judge me this way.* Natalie began to ask the question, "What can I do?"

Natalie took a look at her experience as a technology entrepreneur and began to think about how she could use those skills to create technology that would almost literally help people walk in other people's shoes using tools like virtual reality. She began to believe that with the unique combination of her professional and personal experience, she could scale empathy. Natalie put her voice behind her idea; she shared her personal story and her dream of creating a world of empathy and equality through technology. Then, she took action, launching her new company in 2016. Translator "…is the world's first and only 360° platform for enterprise diversity and inclusion."[23]

Believe

When you are standing at the top of the stairs leading down into a giant auditorium, it is scary as hell to take that first step. An idea and plan on paper is one thing but putting it out into the world, makes it real.

Now that you have the problem in your community that you want to solve and the idea and plan to make that happen, it's time to get to work. This is where my clients often get stuck. In this chapter, you are going to take three key actions that will help propel you and your ideas forward.

When you are standing at the top of the stairs leading down into a giant auditorium, it is scary as hell to take that first step. An idea and plan on paper is one thing but putting it out into the world, makes it real.

One of my clients was going back and forth with her idea for over eight months. Every mentorship call we had together, she started by telling me all the reasons why she hadn't called the people she was supposed to call, launched her website or booked the speaking gigs. She second-guessed her idea and plan constantly, thinking that maybe there was a better way, that maybe she needed to spend more time analyzing and creating documents and spreadsheets. After months of this, I asked her what she thought was holding her back from taking action. She didn't believe 100% that her idea was going to work, and she was waiting for complete certainty before putting herself out there.

This is where it's my job to step in with a reality check. You will never be 100% certain that your idea is going to work. You may fail, but what is much more likely to happen is that you'll have some successes and some failures, and you'll learn from both. More importantly, your idea will get stronger, more solidified and you will start to change lives. You just need to believe a little bit that you can make your dream of creating change in your community (and your life) to get started.

> *What is the price of not taking steps to advance your plan? What will you think in 10 years if you came this far and stopped?*

One of the reasons I made the Women's Changemaker Mentorship™ a group program is because I know that when one of my clients is having a rough day or week and is not succeeding in moving forward, the group, including me, will be there to hold space, as well as some of the fear and doubt, so my client can move forward even though she isn't completely convinced that she can do it.

What is the price of not taking steps to advance your plan? What will you think in 10 years if you came this far and stopped?

I love what the author Elizabeth Gilbert has to say about creative living: "Creative living is choosing the path of curiosity over the path of fear."[24] I have this quote on a sticky note by my computer to remind me that changemaking (and entrepreneurship) is about being creative and curious. There is also a lot of fear involved, whether it's your own mind telling you to stay in your safe career despite your boredom, in the form of hateful words spoken to you at a coffee shop, or in the form of a gun in the hand of a child.

Don't let fear stop you from putting action behind your idea. A big reason why I do this work and care so deeply about helping my clients help more people is I KNOW that you might be sitting on an idea that could be a game changer for millions of people. What if Marie Curie, the scientist who was instrumental in inventing the x-ray, had let fear stop her from pushing her ideas forward?

So, believe in your idea, even if it might change, be curious and find a supportive group of people that can hold your fear for you while you move your ideas into action.

Declare

When I decided to write this book, I immediately announced it to my friends, family and social media communities. I knew that if I announced it, I would probably have to do it. But I also wanted to absorb the excitement and energy my community had for what I was trying to do.

As I mentioned in Chapter 6, one of the first steps I tell my clients to take is to start talking about their changemaking idea. So, now that you have your idea and your plan, if you haven't already, talk to people about it. You don't have to have it all figured out. At the minimum, you can say, "I'm committed to doing something about wildlife conservation. I don't know what I will do yet, but I am going to start learning and figuring out where I can make a difference." People will jump in with their ideas and introductions to people they know or books they've read and off you will go, moving your idea forward.

Act

There is tons of information out there about how to make change, and I'm not saying you shouldn't learn, but you don't need to know everything to take action.

I asked you to make a roadmap so that you will know which direction to head. Start moving. Make one phone call. Take one small action to get your idea moving so that you can start changing your community.

If you don't act, it won't happen, and you will look back in 10 years and wonder, what if?

Get help. Don't try to do this alone. Join a group; get a coach; find a friend to work with you on your idea (or all three).

Don't let information overload lead to paralysis. There is tons of information out there about how to make change, and I'm not saying you shouldn't learn, but you don't need to know everything to take action. *You aren't going to know everything.* And you aren't going to please everyone.

Just start.

If you end up switching gears because your curiosity led you down a more appropriate path for you, that's the beauty of finding your next act, of becoming a Changemaker. You get to explore, switch directions and move toward what intrigues and excites you.

Recently, another client told me that she couldn't seem to take action on her idea of forming a new company to help organizations fundraise. She is a person who normally takes fast action, and so the fact that she was procrastinating was unusual. We spent some time digging into what was holding her back. She told me she just wasn't excited about the work. She knew she could do the work and help a lot of people, but it didn't light her up. I told her that she shouldn't do it then and that we should go back to the drawing board. If you are going to go through the trouble and expense of reinventing yourself, why would you do something that doesn't light you up?

Go Deeper

1. What is the price of not taking steps to put action behind your plan? What will you think in 10 years if you came this far and stopped?

2. Who are three people you will talk to about the change you want to make in your life by creating your next act? What will you tell them?

3. Who are three people you will talk to about your changemaking idea? What will you tell them?

4. What is one action you will take this week to move your idea forward? What are two actions you will take this week? What are five actions you will take in the next month?

5. How will you get help?

CHAPTER 9:

Cultivate Your Legacy

"Legacy: Something transmitted by or received from an ancestor or predecessor or from the past."
– Merriam Webster

Congratulations on taking the first steps to living your legacy and changing your community. I hope you are celebrating the time and energy, both physical and emotional, you chose to put into starting your Changemaker journey.

How are you feeling about your power and ability to create change? Can you see where you might add value and fill a gap in your community?

Every single one of the people whose stories I shared in this book started their journey with an idea. The only differences between them and you are the actions they have already taken and the time they have already dedicated to move their better-world idea forward.

They also shared several things in common when it came to launching their business, organization or passion project:

- They took action
- They moved forward despite not knowing the exact right steps and being afraid
- They invested in their ideas and themselves
- They got help

Remember Ruth, from Chapter 1, who turned the sudden end of her career and the loss of her mother into a company helping people with Alzheimer's and dementia recall memories? In this chapter, we talked about how reinventing yourself into a Changemaker isn't about starting over. It's about building on what you've already accomplished. It's about stretching yourself to create a career and life that you are excited about and that fits you.

In Chapter 2, we saw how Toni Maloney didn't sit back and do nothing after 9/11. She launched the Business Council for Peace that 15 years later is impacting the lives of tens of thousands of people in conflicted, affected countries and is helping to create safer communities. In this chapter, you learned what a Changemaker is and how you can use your own story of reinvention to help create powerful change in your life and community.

In Chapter 3, Dianne Grossman's story of how she founded Mallory's Army™ showed you how a person can turn an unimaginable personal tragedy into a catalyst for change to bring awareness to and help end the culture of bullying. In this chapter, you picked the issue you want to put your energy behind; you learned about the different types of Changemakers; and why it's important to start with your own community.

In Chapter 4, Desiree Adaway gave us a great example of why it is so important to claim your vision and understand your motivations for working toward that vision.

In Chapter 5, you learned how important it is to understand the issue you are focused on, from all sides of the issue. I introduced the Theory of Change and how you can use it to build out your better-world idea. In this chapter, you were inspired by and learned from the stories of Dayna Reggero, Founder of the Climate Listening Project; Pavni Guharoy, Founder of ImpactLens Photography; and my client, Maria, who worked with me to start a community center in her town.

In Chapter 6, you learned, in part from my mistakes, how important it is to map your stakeholders and choose your beneficiaries. You also looked at why building a supportive team around you is important.

In Chapter 7, you learned from Marie's community center how to develop your own roadmap for your changemaking initiative. I also gave you some solid advice on how you think about money and funding in relation to changemaking. I also provided some alternatives to put legal structure around your idea.

Finally, in Chapter 8, you learned about Natalie Egan, who, obsessed with solving the problem of inequality after coming out as a transgender woman, founded Translator to use technology to create diversity and inclusion. You learned the three key principles that you need to adopt to go from having an idea that sits in your head to giving it life, so it creates change in our world. Believe. Declare. Act.

After reading these stories and answering the Go Deeper questions at the end of each chapter, can you see more clearly the path you can take to create change in your life and community?

What to Do Now

Years ago, I met the director of a women's shelter in Connecticut at a networking event. To say she was impressive is putting it lightly; she had a post-graduate degree in systems engineering, was bilingual, and moved with extreme ease through the crowd, capturing each person she spoke to with her personality. I thought *this woman could be doing anything. She could be anything.* So, I asked her what makes her dedicate her talent and time to the women's shelter, instead of to a high-paying corporate job? She told me, "I want to be in love with my life. I don't want to have a lukewarm affair. I want head-spinning, stomach-flipping love. This job gives me that."

For her, love was found in helping women at their most vulnerable moments. It wasn't easy work. Her job had its share of ups and downs. But at the end of the day, she loved it. I believe you should have this love in your life.

When I originally had the idea to write this book, I wanted to do it because I was told it would be a good way to promote my work. My first title was very matter of fact. *Next Act, Give Back: How to Build a Non-profit, Social Enterprise or Foundation.* Then, I started to interview people about what giving back means to them. One of the questions I asked was, "On a scale of one to ten, how important is giving back to you?" Ninety-five percent of the interviewees responded with at least a 10; some even said 11. So many of the people I interviewed had fantastic ideas for businesses that would help create healthy food systems, foundations and investment funds that would move money toward promoting the advancement of women, and community initiatives that create more inclusive learning environments in public schools. And so many told me that their legacy was very important to them.

But there was a disconnect between what people were telling me and what they were doing. They told me how important giving back was to them and that they wanted their legacy to be something greater than running a business or managing a career. Several told me how unfulfilled they were in their current path but that they felt stuck. Then they told me all the reasons why they couldn't take action on their idea. "I don't know enough about the issues." "There are so many problems in the world; what's the point?" "I don't have the money, time, energy, brains, personality, etc."

Sure, some of the people I interviewed were just telling me what they thought I wanted to hear. That they strongly believe in giving back, they donate some money at the end of the year to charities and they volunteer sometimes. I have to admit, that I reached a point in my interviews where I seriously considered calling this book, *F*** Charity, Make Change!* Not because I don't like charitable organizations, I do! It's just that I know when you go beyond giving a few bucks to charity, when you put your energy, time and ideas into making change, you will not only feel powerful and impactful, you will change your life, and you'll help heal your community.

That's why I wrote this book. I want to help you find your path to creating a life that you are head over heels in love with through changemaking. I want you to live your legacy so that you can be even more proud of and fulfilled by your life and you can help make our communities safer, healthier and more just. I want to help you use your voice and your story to pull your ideas out of your head and into the world.

I am not saying you must quit your job or empty your bank account. I am not saying you have to come out of retirement or neglect your kids. I am not saying there is one right way to live your legacy and change your community.

I am saying that you are the one who has to take the first step.

If you are curious about how you can use your next act to give back and make transformative change in your life and community, let's talk about how you can become a part of my community of Changemakers. My promise to you is that I will always be there to help you use your brilliance, power and passion to change lives. If you have already decided that you are ready to take action, or you need to talk it out with someone, I'm here for you. My goal is to help you help your community.

Don't look back in 10 years and wish you had done something today to change your life.

Someday is now.

References

1. " ." Mark Leibowitz Photography Inc. | Certified B Corporation. Accessed September 18, 2018. https://bcorporation.net/.

2. "B Corporation (certification)." Wikipedia. August 13, 2018. Accessed September 18, 2018. https://en.wikipedia.org/wiki/B_Corporation_(certification).

3. "It's Time to Do This." Ellevest. Accessed September 18, 2018. https://www.ellevest.com/impact-investing.

4. Seither, Marci. *Empty Nest: Strategies to Help Your Kids Take Flight.* Kansas City, MO: Beacon Hill Press of Kansas City, 2014.

5. "About Our Founder." Improving Working Conditions for Women through Social Goodness. Accessed September 18, 2018. https://www.workingforwomen.org/founder/.

6. "Theory of Change." Improving Working Conditions for Women through Social Goodness. Accessed September 18, 2018. https://www.workingforwomen.org/theory-of-change/.

7. "Working for Women has a Dual Mission to Enable Businesses to Be a Force for Social Good and Elevate Women in the Workforce." Improving Working Conditions for Women through Social Goodness. Accessed September 18, 2018. https://www.workingforwomen.org/.

8. "Why Are Old People Less Scared of Dying?" Time. Accessed September 18, 2018. http://time.com/4217039/why-are-old-people-less-scared-of-dying/.

9. "Welcome." Women For Progress. Accessed September 18, 2018. https://womenforprogress.org/.

10. Clendaniel, Morgan, and Morgan Clendaniel. "What Is A Changemaker?" Fast Company. August 04, 2016. Accessed September 18, 2018. https://www.fastcompany.com/3062483/what-is-a-Changemaker.

11. "Kinona Is Putting The Lifestyle Into Golf Fashion." Women & Golf Magazine. Accessed September 18, 2018. https://womenandgolf.com/fashion/what-s-new-in-golf-fashion/5692-kinona-is-putting-the-lifestyle-into-golf-fashion.

12. Sharma, Monica. *Radical Transformational Leadership: Strategic Action for Change Agents.* Berkeley, CA: North Atlantic Books, 2017.

13. "Criterion Institute." Criterion Institute. Accessed September 18, 2018. http://www.criterioninstitute.org/.

14. "Sustainable Wealth Management." Veris Wealth Partners. Accessed September 18, 2018. http://www.veriswp.com/.

15. "Dove Self-Esteem Project." Dove US. January 11, 2016. Accessed September 18, 2018. https://www.dove.com/us/en/dove-self-esteem-project.html.

16. STEM Like a Girl. Accessed September 18, 2018. http://stemlikeagirl.org/.

17. Buckley, Dylan. "9 Types of Motivation That Make It Possible to Reach Your Dreams." Lifehack. September 04, 2018. Accessed September 18, 2018. https://www.lifehack.org/articles/productivity/6-types-of-motivation-explained.html.

18. "Power | Definition of Power in English by Oxford Dictionaries." Oxford Dictionaries | English. Accessed September 18, 2018. https://en.oxforddictionaries.com/definition/power.

19. "Home." Hot Bread Kitchen. September 04, 2018. Accessed September 18, 2018. https://hotbreadkitchen.org/.

20. "Incubates." Hot Bread Kitchen. April 17, 2018. Accessed September 18, 2018. https://hotbreadkitchen.org/incubates/.

21. "What Is a Foundation? | Knowledge Base." GrantSpace. Accessed September 18, 2018. https://grantspace.org/resources/knowledge-base/what-is-a-foundation/.

22. "B Corporation (certification)." Wikipedia. August 13, 2018. Accessed September 18, 2018. https://en.wikipedia.org/wiki/B_Corporation_(certification).

23. "Translator." Translator. Accessed September 18, 2018. https://translator.company/.

24. "Elizabeth Gilbert - Choosing Curiosity Over Fear." The On Being Project. Accessed September 18, 2018. https://onbeing.org/programs/elizabeth-gilbert-choosing-curiosity-over-fear/.

Organizations and Companies Referenced in this Book

Aid to Artisans

Ashoka

Barro Sin Plomo

Black Lives Matter

Business Council for Peace (Bpeace)

Climate Listening Project

Councilwoman Kathy O'Keefe

Criterion Institute

Dhana, Inc

Dining for Women

Essential Awakenings

EYElliance

First Tee

Folia Water

Global Goods Partners

Hot Bread Kitchen

ImpactLens Photography

Jam Program

Khan Academy

Kinona Sport

Kuña

LASER International

Mallory's Army™ Foundation

Museum of the Courageous

Oakland Peace Center

One Refugee Child

Stem Like a Girl

Stephanie Lawrence Initiatives

Teach for All

Teach for America

The Adaway Group

Translator

True Ridge Foundation

Veris Wealth Partners

VisionSpring

Women for Progress

Working for Women

About the Author

Kirsten grew up in Apalachin, New York, and is the middle daughter of two school teachers. From an early age, her parents taught her what it means to be a caring, contributing member of the community. Giving back wasn't a term she heard very often growing up. It was so ingrained in the culture of her family that there was no need to give it a special label.

Kirsten's dreams were too big for a small town. When her parents asked her what she wanted to celebrate her high school graduation, she replied, "a plane ticket." Kirsten left to spend a year in Finland as an exchange student, and she hasn't stopped traveling since.

She started her career as a program director for a student exchange organization. When that didn't pay the bills, she took jobs in the fashion industry and in the international banking sector in New York

City. She also lived and worked in Costa Rica, developing programs for volunteers and traveling throughout Central America selling jewelry and handcrafts to tourists.

Using her Spanish language skills, she landed in the international non-profit sector working for organizations such as Aid to Artisans, EastWest Institute, Rainforest Alliance, Trickle Up and VisionSpring.

After a 20-year career in global development, where she fundraised over $20 million and designed and managed social change programs in 10 countries, Kirsten reinvented herself and invented the Women's Changemaker Mentorship™, a one-of-a-kind program that propels successful women to use their next act to become Changemakers in their communities.

Kirsten is also the creator of the original story series, *Ordinary, Extraordinary Changemakers*, which documents the lives of ordinary people making extraordinary change in their communities. Her writings on philanthropy, non-profits and social enterprise have been published in *Forbes* and *Huff Post*. She's been a guest on numerous podcasts including *The Mind Aware Show*. She has been the speaker at conferences including the Women as Change Makers conference in Reno, Nevada.

She lives with her wife, two dogs and three cats on the top of a mountain in northern New Jersey, an hour outside of New York City.

How to Work with Kirsten

Kirsten typically works with successful women who are at a reflection point in their career and are curious about how they can use their next act to give back but aren't sure what to do or how to do it. She believes in the power of harnessing the under-tapped skills, networks and ideas of midcareer women to create a better world.

Through Kirsten's *Women's Changemaker Mentorship™*, she helps her clients find their path to live a legacy of helping create healthier, safer and more equitable communities. Many of her clients start heart-centered businesses, organizations and community initiatives, while other clients repurpose their skills to join existing organizations and programs. This is where her vision, mission, skills, experience and passion collide to create her superpower: helping people help more people.

After many years working across cultures and time zones, Kirsten is accustomed to working with people all over the world. She designed the Women's Changemaker Mentorship™ to be a mostly online, live program so that people in all communities, with all abilities, will have the opportunity to become Changemakers in their communities.

To get on Kirsten's calendar to see if you are a good fit to work with her, go to www.kirstenbunch.com/call.

Acknowledgments

Thank you to every one of the 50+ people who agreed to be interviewed for this book. Your life stories and aspirations made this book robust and relatable. Thank you to each one of my clients, past and present, who trust me to help guide them along their reinvention and Changemaker journey. Thank you to my Book Launch Team who kept me laughing when times got tough, helped me make key decisions about this book, and kept me true to my vision. Thank you to Hilary, my editor, who was the first person to tell me that my book was "written for her." Thank you to the FEMMs who provide me support, advice and encouragement on my journey to make my vision for better communities a reality. Thank you to Desiree, Jenn and Robyn who were my coaches over the past few years and helped show me to the path of my own reinvention. Thank you to my friends who continue to tell me I am a gift, even when I feel like I'm not. Thank you to Piere d'Arterie for turning my vision for the images in this book into deeply moving illustrations. Thank you to all of the people whose stories I share in this book. You inspire me every day. Finally, thank you to my wife for always being my rock.